Food Co-operatives in Turkey

This book addresses the roles played by food co-operatives in the attempt to build alternative food networks, drawing on an in-depth analysis of case studies in Turkey.

While many existing studies focus on food co-operatives and alternative food networks in the Global North, this book provides an important insight into a country from the Global South and, in doing so, not only provides a novel perspective but also challenges the rigid North–South categorization. The book provides a rounded view by examining both a producer and a consumer co-operative: BÜKOOP is a university-based consumer food co-operative, and the Vakıflı co-operative is a food-producing co-operative located in the Hatay province on the Mediterranean coast of Turkey. These two co-operatives, which have been working together for more than ten years, share the dream of establishing a network of co-operatives, in which producers exist in solidarity with consumers, blurring the dichotomy of producer versus consumer as well as rural versus urban. In addition to contributing towards a better understanding of the urban–rural divide, within the framework of alternative food networks, the in-depth analysis of these two cases enables us to explore how food co-operatives develop and how they keep their commitment to their original goals and ideals so as to help build an alternative food system. The lessons we learn from these two working case examples highlight the successes and areas of improvement for food co-operatives. They also provide evidence against the pessimism about alternative food networks by demonstrating that co-operatives can democratize both production and consumption.

This book will be of interest to students and scholars studying alternative food networks, food justice, food sovereignty, transformation towards sustainable food systems, social movements, and the urban–rural divide.

Özlem Öz is Professor of Organization Studies at Boğaziçi University, Turkey. She won the Turkish Academy of Sciences' 'Successful Young Scientists Award' and 'Encouragement Award in Social Sciences and Humanities,' and was the co-winner of the 2018 Best Article Prize of the *International Journal of Urban and Regional Research*. She is the author of many articles and two books, *The Competitive Advantage of Nations: The Case of Turkey* (1999) and *Clusters and Competitive Advantage: The Turkish Experience* (2004).

Zühre Aksoy is Associate Professor of Political Science and International Relations at Boğaziçi University, Turkey. She has authored several book chapters and articles in journals including *Global Environmental Politics*, *Journal of Rural Studies*, and *Food, Culture & Society*. She is a lead author in the Intergovernmental Science-Policy Platform on Biodiversity and Ecosystem Services (IPBES) Transformative Change Assessment (2022–2025).

Routledge Focus on Environment and Sustainability

Regional Political Ecologies and Environmental Conflicts in India
Edited by Sarmistha Pattanaik and Amrita Sen

Circular Economy and the Law
Bringing Justice into the Frame
Feja Lesniewska and Katrien Steenmans

Land Tenure Reform in Sub-Saharan Africa
Interventions in Benin, Ethiopia, Rwanda, and Zimbabwe
Steven Lawry, Rebecca McLain, Margaret Rugadya, Gina Alvarado, and Tasha Heidenrich

Agricultural Digitization and Zhongyong Philosophy
Creating a Sustainable Circular Economy
Yiyan Chen, Hooi Hooi Lean, and Ye Li

EU Trade-Related Measures against Illegal Fishing
Policy Diffusion and Effectiveness in Thailand and Australia
Edited by Alin Kadfak, Kate Barclay, and Andrew M. Song

Food Cultures and Geographical Indications in Norway
Atle Wehn Hegnes

Sustainability and the Philosophy of Science
Jeffry L. Ramsey

Food Co-operatives in Turkey
Building Alternative Food Networks
Özlem Öz and Zühre Aksoy

For more information about this series, please visit: www.routledge.com/Routledge-Focus-on-Environment-and-Sustainability/book-series/RFES

Food Co-operatives in Turkey
Building Alternative Food Networks

Özlem Öz and Zühre Aksoy

Routledge
Taylor & Francis Group
LONDON AND NEW YORK

earthscan
from Routledge

First published 2024
by Routledge
4 Park Square, Milton Park, Abingdon, Oxon OX14 4RN

and by Routledge
605 Third Avenue, New York, NY 10158

Routledge is an imprint of the Taylor & Francis Group, an informa business

© 2024 Özlem Öz and Zühre Aksoy

The right of Özlem Öz and Zühre Aksoy to be identified as authors of
this work has been asserted in accordance with sections 77 and 78 of the
Copyright, Designs and Patents Act 1988.

British Library Cataloguing-in-Publication Data
A catalogue record for this book is available from the British Library

ISBN: 978-1-032-26627-5 (hbk)
ISBN: 978-1-032-26628-2 (pbk)
ISBN: 978-1-003-28916-6 (ebk)

DOI: 10.4324/9781003289166

Typeset in Times New Roman
by Apex CoVantage, LLC

To our parents;
To the volunteers of BÜKOOP and Vakıflı;
and to İdil;
for a better future . . .

Contents

Preface   *viii*

1   Theoretical and contextual framework   1

2   The experience of a consumer food co-op: BÜKOOP   28

3   The experience of a producer food co-op: Vakıflı co-op   47

4   Conclusions and implications   67

Index   *82*

Preface

When Routledge approached us to ask whether or not we would be interested to write a book on food co-operatives in Turkey based on our article (which was published in 2019 in *Food, Culture & Society*) about BÜKOOP, a university-based consumer food co-operative established in Istanbul in 2009, we felt very excited and encouraged. We were both amongst the founders of BÜKOOP, working with our dear co-operator friends towards the dream of strengthening the consumers and producers simultaneously, seeing it as part of a struggle to create an alternative to the existing relations of production and consumption so that transformation towards a just and sustainable food system could ultimately be attained. BÜKOOP inspired the foundation of other food co-ops both in Istanbul and in other parts of the country, and the experience of BÜKOOP, we believe, is important for diverse reasons. First of all, it speaks to the literature on alternative food movements and on food co-ops, providing insights regarding challenges of building alternatives and how to deal with them. When we analysed the case of BÜKOOP in this light, we identified the following crucial dimensions of the issue: how to handle the tension between 'dreams' and 'practical necessities' of running an organization; costs and benefits related to scale (i.e., whether small is indeed beautiful); processes through which co-op spirit is developed and maintained; and what it means to be a 'successful' consumer food co-op. The latter, that is, the meaning of success for a consumer food co-op, is particularly associated by the volunteers of BÜKOOP with its capacity to survive without sacrificing the original goals and ideals of the co-op. This capacity has become even more pronounced in recent years, which unfortunately brought a series of severe crises, one after the other. BÜKOOP had to face and tackle them, and its resilience, it seems, owes a lot to the determinism and emotional attachment of its members, its volunteers, and consumers of the co-op. The volunteers in particular much emphasize the therapeutic role of working together in BÜKOOP. A final note here relates to the fact that we as the authors are amongst the founders and volunteers of BÜKOOP, giving us an opportunity to speak from 'within' regarding all these interesting issues about consumer food co-ops, a side benefit of which is to provide contributions to the growing literature on analytic auto-ethnography.

Therefore, we felt that this valuable and inspiring experience should be shared, complete with an updated discussion of BÜKOOP's story presented in our previous article in *Food, Culture & Society* (2019). Furthermore, we also felt that to be able to provide a full picture, a detailed analysis of a producer food co-op that BÜKOOP works with must be included in the book. We picked the Vakıflı co-operative for this purpose, which is a women's co-op located in the Hatay Province on the Mediterranean coast of Turkey. BÜKOOP and Vakıflı have been working together since BÜKOOP's foundation in 2009 (Vakıflı women's co-op's history goes back to 2005), that is, for a full 14-year period, making it possible to better understand specific dynamics of this mutual relationship between a consumer and a producer food co-op. In addition, Vakıflı as a case not only presents opportunities to explore the challenges, achievement, and ambivalences of producer food co-ops but also enables us to study two additional dimensions of the issue. Firstly, it is a women's co-op, generating insights as to the ways producer food co-ops might empower women economically, socially, and psychologically. Secondly, it provides opportunities to analyse the role co-operatives might play in community development, especially given that this village, like many others in rural Anatolia, risks losing its population to migration to big cities. The fact that Vakıflı is the last remaining village of the Armenian community in Anatolia perhaps makes this dimension even more pronounced in their case, leading to a strong identification with their co-op in terms of intergenerational continuity of ways of life and village livelihoods.

We should perhaps underline, at this juncture, that in this book, we had many instances (perhaps far too many than we would have preferred to, given the number and magnitude of the crises these two co-ops unfortunately had to face in recent years) to analyse extensively how BÜKOOP and Vakıflı responded to and survived the crises that they faced. This opportunity to study their remarkable resilience in turn enabled us to muse further about the concept of 'success' in the case of food co-ops. What accounts for their success, we argue, does speak volumes for the possibilities and the likely paths for the transformation towards a just and sustainable food system, as we discuss in detail in the concluding part of this book.

The book mainly targets an academic audience. The core concepts of the book revolve around understanding and theorizing food co-ops at the nexus of the urban–rural divide. The ultimate purpose is to contribute towards the key question of how we can empower consumers and producers simultaneously. These are global concerns; hence, all regions and countries are, in fact, amongst the targets. Given the multidisciplinary nature of the subject matter, students (both graduate and senior undergraduate) and scholars from a diverse set of disciplines ranging from environmental studies, political science, political economy of food and agriculture, organization studies, and ecological economics to urban and rural studies may find the book interesting and could benefit not only in their research but also as a course material.

Moreover, although the book mainly addresses an academic audience, the subject matter is also of interest for practitioners and activists as well as decision-/policymakers and planners in governments, international organizations, and NGOs seeking to develop a fair and more sustainable food system.

We would like to acknowledge that the research for this book is supported by BAP Project No. 19464, Boğaziçi University. We would also like to thank *Food, Culture & Society* for the permission to reuse in this book a revised and updated version of our article on BÜKOOP published in that journal in 2019 (Ref: Öz, Ö., & Aksoy, Z. (2019). Challenges of Building Alternatives: The Experience of a Consumer Food Co-operative in Istanbul. *Food, Culture & Society*, 22(3), 299–315; copyright © The Association for the Study of Food & Society (ASFS), reprinted by permission of Taylor & Francis Ltd, http://www.tandfonline.com on behalf of The Association for the Study of Food & Society). Our thanks also go to our interviewees from both BÜKOOP and Vakıflı for openly and sincerely sharing their views with us. We, in fact, would like to send our heartfelt thanks to all volunteers of BÜKOOP and Vakıflı for their admirable and inspiring work and efforts, despite all odds, which gives us genuine hope that a much better world is possible. This book is dedicated to them, to our parents, and to Zühre's daughter İdil for a better future.

Özlem Öz & Zühre Aksoy
Istanbul

1   Theoretical and contextual framework

This book addresses the role food co-ops play in the efforts to build a fair and sustainable food system. Based on an in-depth analysis of two case examples from Turkey, the book explores the accomplishments, prospects, and challenges that might emerge in the attempt to create alternatives within the framework of diverse economies and alternative food networks (AFNs). The two cases analysed in detail in the book to achieve this undertaking are, firstly, a university-based consumer food co-operative in Istanbul (Boğaziçi Members Consumer Co-operative, BÜKOOP hereafter) and, secondly, a producer co-op (Vakıfköy Women's Enterprise, Production, and Management Co-operative, Vakıflı co-op hereafter) in Vakıflı, Antakya, located on the Mediterranean coast of Turkey. The latter co-op initially (between 2005 and 2021) functioned as the women's branch of Vakıflı Village Agro-Development Co-operative (Vakıflı agriculture co-op hereafter) and was established in 2021 as an official women's co-op (i.e., Vakıfköy Women's Enterprise, Production, and Management Co-operative). BÜKOOP and the Vakıflı co-op, which have been working together for about 14 years, share the dream of establishing a network of co-operatives, in which producer co-operatives would be in solidarity with consumer co-operatives. In addition to contributing towards a better understanding of the urban–rural divide within the framework of AFNs, the in-depth analysis of these two co-ops enables us to explore how a food co-op develops and keeps its commitment to its original goals and ideals so as to help build an alternative food system, given the external and internal challenges and ambivalences. The lessons we learn from these two working case examples highlight the facts, possibilities, and areas of improvement for food co-ops and demonstrate that co-operatives can democratize both production and consumption.

One central concern of the study revolves around the debate on the presence and the handling of the tension between 'ideals' and 'practical necessities' within the literature on diverse economies. For the two cases covered in the book, the question of how to balance ideals and everyday exigencies of running an organization has been a central concern. Relatedly, whether or not or how much a food co-op needs to grow has been another crucial question for these co-ops, whose experiences have important implications for the debates

DOI: 10.4324/9781003289166-1

on de-growth. The study reveals and discusses the facts and possibilities for food co-ops in light of the analyses conducted with a particular emphasis on how emerging issues – namely, how to handle the tension between 'ideals' and 'practical necessities'; whether small is indeed beautiful; and the meanings and realizations of 'co-op spirit' and 'success' – echo at both ends, especially with regard to the conditions associated with the ideal of empowering producers and consumers simultaneously, providing implications for urban–rural connections, and discussions about the possibilities of multi-stakeholder co-operatives (MSCs). By making comparisons with other settings in the global North and the South when relevant, the study also provides a discussion as to how the results derived from an in-depth analysis of the two cases studied from Turkey resonate *vis-à-vis* the available literature.

The two cases covered in the study constitute working examples towards their ideals, providing evidence against the pessimism about alternative economic organizations in general and alternative food movement in particular. Although challenges are significant, achievements of these two co-ops are very inspiring with important implications, as food co-ops constitute an institutionalized form of interaction between consumers and producers. This in turn provides some degree of control over the agricultural production and consumption process, which is extremely limited in the dominant food system. With an in-depth analysis of two co-operatives in Turkey, the study discusses whether/how food co-ops provide a framework for resilience and justice for their members and what implications can be drawn from these examples for the transformation of the dominant food system.

In this introductory chapter, we present the theoretical and contextual framework of our study on co-operatives as an organizational form of AFNs, and the historical development and the current state of producer and consumer food co-ops in Turkey. The chapter explores the role that co-operatives play in changing the dynamics of production and consumption in light of the debate about the potentials and constraints of AFNs in transforming food politics. The discussions in the chapter are linked to relevant debates in the literature, which are then reflected in the Turkish experience, detailing how the agricultural and food co-operative model is developing in Turkey.

With the resurgence of neoliberalism, argues Gibson-Graham (2003, 126), we witness "the naturalization of the view that we have no (longer a) role in making and managing the economy." However, this depiction of 'a malevolent beast of capitalism' is neither empirically accurate nor politically useful (Sharpe, 2014, 29). Instead, there is a need for redefining economy as a heterogeneous space that actors with widely differing roles, power structures, and interlinkages can shape, which leaves room for the democratization of economy via political interventions.

Alternatives, however, need to address the issue of economic organization precisely because economic organization is not a 'given' but constructed. This requires a holistic approach that involves the organization of alternative forms of production, distribution, and consumption: Embedded in the social and ecological, and involving different forms of collective ownership and self-management practices (Adaman and Akbulut, 2016, 38). The debate on de-growth is importantly pertinent for this endeavour, as it challenges the fixation on growth in multiple forms it can take and entails re-thinking economy "firstly by foregrounding democratic choices and debates in the shaping of the economy, and secondly by re-imagining economic relations and identities in different terms" (Fournier, 2008, 532). Co-operatives as solidarity organizations have the potential to address these concerns and, hence, to start building alternatives *now*.

ICA (The International Co-operative Alliance) defines a co-operative as "an autonomous association of persons united voluntarily to meet their common economic, social, and cultural needs and aspirations through a jointly owned and democratically controlled enterprise" (ICA, 2022). Co-operatives are more prevalent than often assumed. The ICA reports that more than 800 million people in the world are organized into co-operatives, and co-ops provide over 100 million jobs around the world; in fact, "at least 12% of humanity is a co-operator of any of the 3 million co-operatives on earth" (ICA, 2022). More than 20% of New Zealand's GDP is, for example, generated by co-operatives, whereas the corresponding figure is 37% of Brazil's agricultural GDP (Reyes and Harnecker, 2013, 25).

The chapter situates the Turkish case within the discussion of AFNs and co-operatives in the Global North and South. The study of AFNs and co-ops in Turkey presents an excellent opportunity to explore and unfold common features of and differences in both contexts: Firstly, in terms of the similarities that can be identified with respect to the structure of agriculture and development of co-ops in the northern Mediterranean context; and secondly, in terms of its embeddedness in many problems that the food and agriculture sectors of countries in the global South currently face. As such, the chapter problematizes a strict divide between the 'developed North' and the 'developing South' in the context of AFNs and food co-ops. To this end, it is structured in three subsections, covering firstly, alternative food movements and networks; secondly, challenges for food co-ops as collectivist-democratic organizations; and thirdly, by an overview and discussion of co-ops and AFNs in the Turkish context.

Alternative food movements and networks

The contemporary food system is increasingly characterized by the consolidation of corporate power, which affects every single stage of the food supply chain from production to consumption (Clapp, 2022, 45). Thereby, an important challenge is the increased marginalization of small farmers and consumers. A recent International Panel of Experts on Sustainable Food Systems (IPES) report states that "more than 50% of farmers and rural workers live below the poverty line in several countries in the Global South with the largest rural populations" (IPES-Food, 2020, 4–5). The situation is no less daunting on the consumer side: "Almost 3.1 billion people could not afford a healthy diet in 2020, an increase of 112 million more people than in 2019" (FAO et al., 2021, xix). The long-standing fragility of the food system has become all the more apparent with COVID-19, vividly demonstrating that "food is not a commodity like any other" (IPES-Food, 2020, 5).

It is in this context that we see, in the past 30 years, a growing number of AFNs to address the problems created by the dominant food system. In parallel, a significant scholarship has also emerged since the late 1990s analysing these movements (Whatmore and Thorne, 1997; Allen et al., 2003; Renting et al., 2003; Goodman et al., 2012). One of the earlier accounts of AFNs is by Feenstra (1997), defining them as structures that "aim to be economically viable for farmers and consumers, use ecologically sound production and distribution practices, and enhance social equity and democracy for all members of the community" (Feenstra, 1997, 28). Jarosz (2008, 232) states that

> AFNs are defined in four major ways: (1) by shorter distances between producers and consumers; (2) by small farm size and scale, and organic or holistic farming methods, which are contrasted with large scale, industrial agribusiness; (3) by the existence of food purchasing venues such as food co-operatives, farmers' markets, and CSA, and local food-to-school linkages; (4) by a commitment to the social, economic, and environmental dimensions of sustainable food production, distribution, and consumption.

The now rich literature on AFNs analyses these movements in terms of their place and impact in the dominant industrial food system, applying a variety of theoretical perspectives and a number of case studies. Looking at several definitions of AFNs, Forssell and Lankoski (2015, 66) find three anchors from which AFNs are viewed: First is a focus on food itself and its production process; second is the organization of food supply; and finally, the participant actors who make up the network. Nevertheless, one common point authors find in these AFN definitions is that they are posited as different from the 'conventional' food networks (Forssell and Lankoski, 2015, 66).

In discussing diverse economies, Gibson-Graham (2008, 615) highlights the significance of "representing and documenting the huge variety of economic transactions, labour practices and economic organizations that contribute to social well-being worldwide," in which Gibson-Graham includes consumer, producer, and worker co-operatives, and community-supported agriculture, amongst others. Within the growing number of AFNs, co-operatives occupy a central role. Challenges posed by fierce market competition and rising food prices are important in making these networks a crucial part of the search for access to good and quality food at reasonable prices, while supporting small-scale producers. As food co-ops "pioneered many prac- tices currently associated with the alternative food movement" (Zitcer, 2015, 812), they are directly related to the debate on AFNs. A close examination of different types of AFNs can provide insights on the "debate about alterity and diverse economies issues together with contradictions between inten- tions and practices" (Gritzas and Kavoulakos, 2016, 927). Therefore, analys- ing food co-ops can be particularly revealing to comprehend the different degrees of alterity they present, and the possibilities and limits of building alternatives.

In addition to making alternative forms of economic organizations more visible, analysis of AFNs can provide novel insights about the potential trans- formation of the people actively involved in them. For example, Sarmiento (2017, 487) underlines multiple scholarly approaches about AFNs which look at how "active involvement with an AFN can expose participants to new ways of thinking about and doing food and food systems." Accordingly, we may ask, for example, how participants' direct involvement with farmers in consumer food co-ops has changed their perceptions regarding building alternatives.

As such, this book analyses co-operatives as part of an AFN research agenda to address the challenges evident in the current food system. Mooney (2004, 86) highlights that co-operatives can play a critical role in shaping "the social relations of production and consumption" (Friedmann, 1995, cited in Mooney, 2004, 86). AFNs are crucial in their quest to provide alternatives that require a fundamental rethinking of farmer–consumer relations. For example, Parkins and Craig (2009, 79) underline AFN's potential of linking farmers and consumers in direct ways that are likely to facilitate trust. Relatedly, Qazi and Selfa (2005, 47) note the importance of comprehending the politics of pro- duction and consumption to be able to "theorize about the active, relational, and political role of consumers along with producers in the development of alternative food provisioning." Rethinking producer–consumer relations that problematize existing global food system's feature of 'distancing' producers and consumers includes discussions on alternative food supply chains, such as short food supply chains (SFSCs) (Renting et al., 2003; Marsden and Smith, 2005), and Hergesheimer and Wittman's (2012, 376) discussion of "socially embedded 'grain chain'," amongst others. The cases of BÜKOOP and Vakıflı we analyse not only demonstrate what it means to be 'active consumers and producers' but also open a rich discussion regarding the specifics of establish- ing and maintaining such direct links between farmers and consumers, as we will discuss in the following pages.

As AFNs take diverse forms, there is a growing debate in scholarly lit- erature about how to categorize them. Tregear (2011) underscores this multi- plicity, for example, pointing to the categorization by Allen et al. (2003), as alternative or oppositional; by Watts et al. (2005), as strong or weak; and by Renting et al. (2003), as territorial versus ecological; amongst others (cited in Tregear, 2011, 424). Another categorization is based on 'Multi-actor Perspective' (MaP), according to which AFNs are clustered as "consumer-led, third-sector-led, business platforms, farmer-led, public-led, and CSAs (collaboration between farmers and consumers)" (Ribeiro et al., 2021, 498). On the other hand, Duncan and Pascucci (2017) provide a typology based on organizational features of AFNs, making a distinction between isomorphic and polymorphic AFNs. Accordingly, they state that "AFNs that organize themselves around community (e.g. sharing knowledge and values) and democratic relations (e.g. shared decision rights and allocation of ownership) can be categorized as polymorphic," an example of which is food co-operatives (Duncan and Pascucci, 2017, 318). This typology is helpful as it unfolds the diverse forms of organizational relations that AFNs can manifest and addresses some of the criticisms about whether these networks are able to challenge the dominant food system. It is to these critiques that we now turn our attention.

In their review of AFNs, Mares and Alkon (2011, 81) analyse the ways they "engage with problematics of inequality and neoliberalism" as two major points that the movement faces criticism. As mentioned earlier, scholarly debate focuses on whether AFNs are oppositional or alternative (Allen et al., 2003; Guthman, 2008) and on different meanings of localism (Allen et al., 2003; DuPuis and Goodman, 2005). In an oft-cited criticism of these networks, Guthman (2008, 1176) posits their limits in challenging the existing food system with a focus on "four recurring themes in contemporary food activism as they intersect with neoliberal rationalities: consumer choice, localism, entrepreneurialism, and self-improvement," and how indeed they "shape the rhetoric and practice of the politically possible." One point that deserves attention is whether AFNs become entrenched in market relations in a way that only serves affluent consumers' demand for healthy and high-quality food, with no benefits for small producers and consumers who cannot afford to access these products (Jarosz, 2008). In addition, a number of studies show the continuity of unequal relations within the production realm, for instance, in terms of farm labour or gender inequities (Allen et al., 2003). Another criticism is proposed by the term 'defensive localism' (Winter, 2003), questioning the progressive agenda of the movements supporting locally produced food.

At the same time, scholars underline the potential of 'co-operative AFNs' to surmount the several constraints of the "more individualistic approaches in the local/sustainable food movement" (Anderson et al., 2014, 3–4). For Anderson et al. (2014, 3–4), 'co-operative AFNs' not only diverge from the major premises of the current food system that endorses competition and maximization of food production but also "create new relational spaces that hold promise for overcoming the pragmatic and political limits of some of the more individualistic approaches in the local/sustainable food movement." Relatedly, Duncan and Pascucci (2017) propose that the very organizational form of AFNs is likely to affect the transformative prospects they will bring. They argue that polyphormic AFNs like food co-operatives are more likely "to advance alternative pathways for transition insofar as their practices are less likely to be taken up by the dominant regime" (Duncan and Pascucci, 2017, 334). Similarly, in a discussion of what alterity entails, Rosol (2020, 55) argues that 'alternative economic practices' should be complementing the AFN components of alternative food products and alternative distribution networks. These practices include

> other forms of economic transactions (e.g. barter, donation, gifting, collecting, production for self-consumption), working practices (e.g. unpaid work of members, equal pay for all employees regardless of rank), forms of economic organization (e.g. co-operatives, collectives), and forms of financing (e.g. member loans, co-operative shares, crowdfunding, and others).
>
> (Rosol, 2020, 59)

In this context, it becomes all the more important to analyse the transformative potential of co-ops like BÜKOOP and Vakıflı as to how they deal with the challenges they face. How exactly are they, for instance, organized? To what extent do they comprise economic practices that could be considered alternative, following Rosol's (2020) conceptualization? How do they approach the issue of growth? Do they consider it an essential step in their development trajectory or see it as a degenerative force damaging co-op spirit, and hence a challenge against being a genuine 'alternative'?

Here, one important point is the difference between earlier food co-ops and the 'new wave' of food co-ops starting in the 1960s and 1970s. Zitcer (2015, 815) underlines that in the United States, earlier food co-ops aimed at providing their members low-priced food, yet while trying to be similar to supermarkets, they not only reduced participation of their members but they were also beaten out by big grocers. New wave co-ops, on the other hand, reflecting the grassroots politics of the period they emerged, gradually "began to incorporate local and organic goods, helping to popularize them in the process" (Zitcer, 2015, 815). In fact, experimentation and innovation leading to different growth paths are at the core of new wave of food co-ops (Little et al., 2010, 1804). For example, Biocoop in France and the Seikatsu Club in Japan, despite comparable ideological positions at the beginning, "evolved into very different organizations relying on different systems of provision" (Little et al., 2010, 1804). An important point is how everyday practicalities and the ways they are negotiated make the co-ops continually in the making (Little et al., 2010, 1811). Another key issue then emerges here regarding food co-ops as to how they might evolve over time and how they can keep their initial ideals given external and internal pressures, and challenges.

Challenges for food co-ops as collectivist-democratic organizations

Mooney (2004, 86–87) asserts that co-operatives embrace the social relations of production and consumption and, thus, have the capability of democratizing both spheres. A major challenge for food co-ops is market competition, which "has pushed co-ops to incorporate the more efficient, but arguably less democratic practices of mainstream supermarkets" (Haedicke, 2012, 44). Haedicke (2012, 56) underlines how, in the natural foods co-op sector, the development of different member labour systems can in part be explained by differences in local markets, yet, perhaps more importantly, it pertains to the debate between co-op members on whether/to what extent "changes in member labour programmes represented an abandonment of co-operative values of economic democracy and community empowerment." Another important pressure on food co-ops comes from competing with retail chains of the grocery industry, which challenge the "decentralized and participatory forms of organization" that characterized the co-op sector (Haedicke, 2012, 57). One implication of this push may be the shift from volunteer member labour to employment of paid workers in the name of increasing efficiency. While many of the challenges that co-ops face are related to the seeming contradiction between their economic and political functions, as Mooney (2004, 81) states, "those very tensions may, in fact, be a wellspring of strength, innovation, and flexibility that, in the long run, serve multiple and sometimes apparently contradictory functions quite well."

Food co-ops continue to be leading alternative organizations, and as such, they serve as a testing ground to analyse the dynamics hidden in the key structure- and process-related issues in alternative organizations. It is crucial to explore the challenges that might emerge in the attempt to build alternatives within the framework of AFNs and diverse economies, and whether and how it is possible to deal with them without sacrificing the original goals. The experiences of BÜKOOP and Vakıflı we analyse in this book aim to provide insights for these important issues, with implications and contributions to the literatures on AFNs and on food co-operatives. The central concern here revolves around the question of how co-ops develop and keep their commitment to original goals and ideals of the co-op as to help build an alternative food system, given external and internal challenges and ambivalences. The aforementioned debate on the presence and the handling of the tension between 'ideals' and 'practical necessities' within the literature on diverse economies, for example, benefits from the experiences of BÜKOOP and Vakıflı. Relatedly, as also mentioned earlier, whether or not or how much the co-op needs to grow has been another crucial question for these two co-ops, whose experiences in this regard have important implications for the debates on de-growth. Schneider et al. (2010, 512) define sustainable de-growth as "equitable downscaling of production and consumption that increases human well-being and enhances ecological conditions at the local and global levels, in the short and long terms." In this context, the analysis of co-ops can provide significant insights about whether/the extent to which they provide the seeds of a future de-growth economy (Kallis et al., 2012, 176). Therefore, it becomes all the more important to analyse the organizational processes that co-ops undergo in dealing with the challenges they face in their efforts to provide an alternative to the dominant food system.

Indeed, although since the time of Owen the focus has largely been on the structures of co-operatives (Stryjan, 1994, 62), we need to focus our analytical lens not only on the structure and its deterioration but also on organizational processes. Co-operatives as a species of organization are constituted by their members, and thus, 'success' of an organization should be seen as the manifestation of an ongoing process of production and re-production of the co-op spirit by these very members, echoing the re-production perspective (Stryjan, 1994). Accordingly, 'members' organizations' are continuously designed and re-designed by their members in a way that shared values have an impact on decisions, which tend to generate organizational routines, organizational routines in turn influencing participants' perceptions, which are then likely to contribute to re-producing and perhaps modifying the routines. Ultimately, all this might collectively reinforce a re-production of membership (Stryjan, 1994, 65).

Rothschild-Whitt (1979) proposes nine conditions that might help a co-op to achieve a collectivist-democratic structure: Internal factors (experimental orientation, mutual and self-criticism, limits to size and alternative growth patterns, economic marginality, dependence on internal support base, technology, and diffusion of knowledge) and external factors (oppositional services and values, supportive professional base, and social movement orientation). 'Experimental orientation' contends that in case of inability to move towards its original goals, an alternative organization may tend towards purposeful self-dissolution. The underlying logic is that it is better for the co-op to disband than to displace its original goals, indicating a clear preference for dissolution over *goal displacement*. The specific dynamics of such dualities and how they could be managed are not well understood in the literature (Ashforth and Reingen, 2014).

'Limits to size and alternative growth patterns' condition underlines that face-to-face relationships and direct democratic forms are hard to maintain if the organization grows beyond a certain size (Rothschild-Whitt, 1979, 222). There is, however, evidence that it might be possible to retain participatory practices as the scale of collective efforts grows, although "compared with larger groups, small ones had fewer difficulties with retaining their participatory-democratic practices and values" (Chen, 2016, 71). While turning into a supermarket (for consumer co-ops) and losing the sense of purpose (for both producer and consumer co-ops) are nightmares for food co-ops, there are healthier ways to grow, such as building a wider network of co-operative relationships with other collectivist organizations or generating spin-offs.

Confirming Rothschild-Whitt's (1979, 227) emphasis on "dependence of an organization on its internal support base," volunteerism is an indispensable feature of many food co-ops. Members volunteer their free time to work at the co-op and to discuss and implement food policies and co-op rules. They in return gain access to natural and organic food and participate "in a worthwhile community and group activity" (Wertheim, 1976, 5). Reliance on volunteers renders them powerful, and in Chen's (2016, 73) words, labour is then "communified" by valuing and integrating members' contributions to the collective, which in turn help prevent alienating members from their work efforts, output, each other, and themselves. In fact, Leach (2016) finds that the most efficient collective groups do avoid paid staff. In a similar vein, the long-term success of food co-operatives is seen to be contingent on the availability and commitment of volunteers (Hibbert et al., 2003). Two noteworthy concerns regarding the issue of volunteerism are problems of free riding and burnout (Paranque and Willmott, 2014). Collectivist work tends to generate less alienation but more stress: Since members "are working for a cause, they are driven to take an overload of work, leading to familiar phenomenon of burnout" (Rothschild-Whitt and Whitt, 1986, 311). In their attempt to build alternatives, therefore, food co-ops face severe challenges from within, and the long-term success of food co-operatives is seen to be particularly contingent on the availability and commitment of volunteers (Hibbert et al., 2003). As we will discuss in the following pages, the issue of volunteerism, including the associated problem of burnout, has been vital for BÜKOOP in its attempt to develop and maintain a co-op spirit, whereas for the case of Vakıflı this issue reveals itself in how the work has been distributed and shared amongst the members.

'Diffusion of knowledge' necessitates the knowledge needed to perform the organization's tasks to be evenly distributed, which has critical implications for power. Relatedly, unevenness in volunteer work can also be considered as a sign of power imbalances. Mansbridge (1979, 194) argues that perhaps the most persistent problem alternative organizations face is their ability to guarantee that every member utilizes equal power in decision-making. In the end, isn't it the founding principle of many co-ops to have 'one member one vote'? It would be hard, however, to state that each member has an equal power in many co-operatives. Just like other forms, co-ops as organizations draw on various coalitions regarding the use of power (Öz and Çalışkan, 2010). Leach (2016, 58) finds that the more efficient collectives tend to be self-reflective in that they "considered it to be each person's responsibility to monitor both their own behaviour and power relations in the group more generally." One argument is that, as knowledge becomes diffused, the possibility that some members will develop exclusive knowledge, with the resulting implications this has for power, declines considerably. This in turn introduces a process of 'demystification' of knowledge, also revealing as well as breaking down any 'pretence of expertise' (Rothschild-Whitt, 1979, 230, 232). The specific dynamics of such processes and how they could be managed are not well understood in the literature (Ashforth and Reingen, 2014), and it is also towards a better understanding of such internal challenges and the specific ways of dealing with them that we hope to contribute based on the experiences of BÜKOOP and Vakıflı.

Another important issue is related to women's roles in AFNs, given the centrality of women to food work (Moon, 2022). According to a survey conducted by the International Labour Organization (ILO) and the International Co-operative Alliance (ICA), "in every region of the world, women's participation in both membership and leadership in co-operatives was significantly below average, especially in the traditionally male-dominated agriculture and finance sectors. This poor participation was especially salient in positions of leadership" (Meliá-Marti et al., 2020, 2). Given that co-operatives are by definition gender-neutral, it is often the cultural issues that pose challenges in this respect, ranging from "social expectations of family responsibilities, personal conflicts of work/family balance," to the lack of know-how and networking opportunities (Meliá-Marti et al., 2020, 2).

Women also form their own co-operatives, which have been a subject of increasing attention in the literature. Sato and Soto Alarcón (2019), for instance, highlight the important role the state has played by providing seed money to a group of women who became founding members of the co-operative in Hidalgo in rural Mexico (Sato and Soto Alarcón, 2019, 48). Kopczyńska (2017, 15), on the other hand, describes the gender-based division of labour in co-ops, women's role typically being limited to dealing with the food itself. Also, there are studies that focus on some related areas such as agro-tourism (e.g., women's co-operative To Kastri in Greece; ILO and ICA, 2014, 7), whereas others look at the consumption side and the class-based dynamics of the issue (e.g., Moon's (2022) analysis of a feminist food co-op in South Korea). Many studies of women's co-ops stress on both economic and non-economic benefits of these co-ops for the women involved, particularly emphasizing the importance of social relations and activities beyond the family (Çınar et al., 2021; Daya and Authar, 2012; Moon, 2022). Given that our second case study, the Vakıflı Co-op, is a women's co-op, its analysis sheds light on different dimensions of the role of co-operatives in women's empowerment, together with associated bottlenecks.

At this point, also part of the debate is co-operatives' role in community development. Gonzales and Philips (2013) point out that the contribution of co-operatives to the communities they are a part of has become all the more important in the current context of and challenges posed by globalization. Majee and Hoyt (2011, 49) define community development "as a process that mobilizes resources and builds the capacity of local residents to work together to improve social and economic conditions in their communities" and underscore the role that co-operatives can play in creating and fostering different forms of capital, including social, human, and financial capital, which are essential in generating community development (Majee and Hoyt,

2011, 51–52). Here, one crucial issue is how co-operatives define their goals, which is also linked to the above discussions about challenges of growth and efficiency. For example, Bijman and Wijers state that "the choice between providing benefits to the whole community versus targeting only member-interests may lead to the exclusion of the poorest and most disadvantaged community members," leading them to conclude that "when producer co-operatives become more market-oriented, they are less likely to be inclusive" (Bijman and Wijers, 2019, 77). The mere existence of a co-operative, there-fore, does not automatically bring community development but is dependent on how goals are defined, as well as on organizational features that are demo-cratic, inclusive, and participatory. The case of Vakıflı we examine in the book provides an excellent opportunity to analyse the potentials of and challenges for co-operatives to bring forth community development.

At the same time, the debate on MSCs is highly relevant for our discussion of the possibilities that the relationship between BÜKOOP, as a consumer co-op, and Vakıflı, as a producer co-op, has built over the years in foster-ing a productive collaboration towards a transformative food politics. Lund (2012, 32) defines MSCs as "co-operatives that formally allow for owner-ship and governance by representatives of two or more 'stakeholder' groups within the same organization. Such co-operatives . . . may include consum-ers, producers, workers, volunteers, and/or general community supporters in their ownership and governance structure." In a similar vein, Gray (2014, 23) asserts that MSCs can address many of the tensions of co-ops we discussed earlier, as well as setting "a community development template for addressing various social, economic, and ecological needs, with a more inclusive and hopefully enduring democratic organization." At the same time, however, one important debate on MSCs is how to bring together the potentially divergent or conflicting interests of multiple stakeholders (i.e., producers and consum-ers) on a common ground that will benefit all. In this context, Ajates Gon-zales (2017, 287) provides a discussion of "more-than-economic-benefits" that MSCs can bring, such as nurturing of social capital, blurring the divide between producers and consumers, and providing space for multiple actors to engage with each another and negotiate, for example, what a 'fair price' is. Ajates (2021, 17) further argues that this 'in-between' space MSCs create is a flexible domain where creativity and reflexivity can nourish: "They exist as work spaces, learning spaces but more noticeably, generating third spaces for co-operation where consumers, workers, buyers, and producers can re-think, produce, and reproduce alternative ways of covering their needs. They are relational, open, internally diverse, and externally stretched." As such, in our in-depth analysis of both BÜKOOP and Vakıflı, we also aim to investigate the questions, potentials, and challenges with regard to MSCs in the context of the relationship they have built with one another over the years and whether the establishment of an MSC would address the tensions and provide possi-bilities for a resilient, just, and sustainable food system.

Finally, in terms of these major issues the book identifies with regard to food co-operatives, one crucial point is whether there are intrinsic differences with regard to AFNs' role within the food systems of the global North and South. While the initial focus of the literature has been on AFNs in the North, there is now considerable body of work that looks at AFNs in the southern context (Freidberg and Goldstein, 2011; Si et al., 2015; Bellante, 2017). Bellante (2017, 121) notes the different structural features of agriculture and food in the North and the South in organic production, for example, the dominance of small-scale peasant agriculture in the South (for whom organic certification requirements are almost prohibitive due to high costs) versus the agribusiness model in the North. This alludes to the importance of alternative certification systems, such as participatory guarantee systems (PGS) in the development of AFNs in the South (Bellante, 2017, 121). Lamine et al. (2012), on the other hand, in their comparison of AFNs in France and Brazil, point out that while there are similarities in terms of the consumer profile in both cases (namely, middle class), there are crucial differences with regard to farmers:

> In France, AFNs are often launched by neo-peasants, most of whom have a higher level of education and/or an urban back-ground. This might facilitate interaction with consumers (even though more rooted farmers may also initiate alternative networks or join in). In Brazil, on the other hand, although many initiatives were also launched by neo-peasants or urban professionals with rural origins, most of them concern family farms and landless farmers, the MST (landless people's movement) being one of the main actors within current alternative movements.
>
> (Lamine et al., 2012, 390)

One important note in this regard is the role played by AFNs in Brazil for the legal recognition of participatory certification (Lamine et al., 2012, 396). As our discussion of BÜKOOP in Chapter 2 will illustrate, the issue of certification has been very important in the choice of farmers for BÜKOOP, many of whom, despite their ecological and organic production, cannot afford to get organic certification. This also has important implications on the consumer side, since organic products in Turkey, as in elsewhere, are considerably more expensive. Therefore, for BÜKOOP, this choice entails supporting agroecological practices of small-scale farmers to sell their produce at fair prices, while also enabling consumers to access high-quality products at affordable prices. Vakıflı provides an illuminating case in this regard, as it started with organic production in the early 2000s, only to later (in 2009) abandon it when it was not economically feasible for the farmers to obtain organic certification. Through an analysis of these two cases of a consumer and a producer co-op in Turkey, where various features of the agriculture and food sector resemble both the North and the South, the book aims to explore whether a strict North–South divide in terms of analysing AFN's role in food systems is a productive path.

All these concerns in turn bring us to a reconsideration of what 'success' means in the context of AFNs and co-operatives. These intertwined issues, namely, how to handle the tension between 'ideals' and 'practical necessities,' whether small is indeed beautiful, and the meanings and realizations of 'co-op spirit' and 'success,' have been perpetual subjects of discussion for BÜKOOP and Vakıflı, revealing also the kinds of ambivalences and challenges faced while building alternatives. As a women's producer co-op in a small village, Vakıflı also provides additional insights regarding possible contributions of co-ops towards women's empowerment and community development. The 14-year-long experience of mutual co-operation of BÜKOOP and Vakıflı, on the other hand, contributes towards a better understanding of how to tackle these key issues, revealing the transformative potential of food co-ops, as will be evident as our analysis unfolds in the following pages. Before proceeding to our case studies, however, we provide an overview of food co-ops and AFNs in the Turkish context in the next section.

Food co-ops and AFNs in Turkey: An overview

Initially more widespread in the North, more recently, AFNs have become an important part of food politics in the Global South. AFNs in Turkey have steadily been increasing since the 2010s. An uneven neo-liberalization of the agriculture sector started in the 1980s in Turkey, gaining momentum after 2000 with the World Bank-assisted Agricultural Reform Implementation Project (ARIP), with the aim to significantly reduce state support for the sector and further integrate it with global markets. The measures included, amongst many others, privatization of state economic enterprises, introduction of direct income support for farmers in order to decouple production and trade, reductions in state subsidies, and reorganization of agricultural co-operatives (Aydın, 2010). Atasoy (2013, 547) states that

> there are two sides to the market intensification of Turkey's agriculture: one concerns the historical centrality of small-scale production directed towards local-regional consumers; the other relates to the increasingly dominant role played by supermarkets through the expansion of agro-industrial food production and supply chains aimed at distant consumers.

While Turkish agriculture has been dominated by small-scale production, an important impact of the neo-liberalization process has been on small producers, reducing their capability to survive in an increasingly competitive market framework. On the other hand, more recently, a significant increase in food prices has been in place, with important implications for low-income households in terms of food consumption. Demirkılıç et al. (2022, 58) note that "coupled with other supply-side problems and the structural problems in the agricultural sector, food prices increased by 20.6% in 2020." According to the World Bank Food Security Update (June 29, 2023), Turkey is within the top ten in the list of food price inflation. In such a context, along with the challenges posed by the pandemic, analysis of agricultural and consumer co-operatives becomes all the more pertinent.

The early 2000s are a turning point for the development of AFNs in Turkey (Ince and Kadirbeyoğlu, 2020). In recent years, the number of new waves of alternative food initiatives, ranging from informal collectives to shopping groups, has indeed increased (Kadirbeyoğlu and Konya, 2017). Taking various forms (community-supported agriculture, food kitchens, community gardens, and food co-ops) along with a diversity of actors participating in these networks, common features of these AFNs include their organization at grassroot levels, being not for profit, and aiming for an alternative framework for producer–consumer relations (Ince and Kadirbeyoğlu, 2020). Relations of trust and mutual support between the producers and consumers are at the core (Öz and Aksoy, 2019; Soysal Al, 2020). For example, Kadıköy Co-op, a consumer co-op established in 2016 in Istanbul, defines the construction of novel connections between producers and consumers based on direct relationship as one of its foundational principles (Kadıköy Kooperatifi Kolektifi, 2020, 163). For these consumer co-ops, one particular focus is the priority given to small producers who are disadvantaged in terms of their capacity to participate in competitive market systems, engaged in ecologically sound and sustainable production practices and committed to the use of local and traditional varieties of crops and seeds. As we will discuss at length in Chapter 2, for BÜKOOP, one of the pioneers of consumer co-ops, this has been a core principle, along with an emphasis on non-exploitative working conditions in farms. In a similar vein, Kadıköy Co-op, for example, emphasizes that the definition of small farmers does not simply refer to scale but rather reflects a production model that is non-exploitative, prioritizes the protection of traditional knowledge and local seeds, does not use pesticides, and does not imitate profit-driven firm behaviour (Kadıköy Kooperatifi Kolektifi, 2020, 164). However, Kadirbeyoğlu and Konya (2017) state that some of the alternative food initiatives they analyse did start with an emphasis solely on having access to healthy food, and then through further engagement and learning in the process, they changed their perspective and goals towards the possibilities of an alternative food system. In addition, we should also note that localization is an important component of these AFNs, with "the spatial organisation of consumers on a neighbourhood scale (e.g. Kadıköy Co-op, Koşuyolu Co-op) or on a university scale (e.g. BÜKOOP). Or consumers may work in collaboration with the producers of a particular local space (e.g. DÜRTÜK's project in Piyalepaşa Bostan)" (Soysal Al, 2020, 138).

While AFNs are a relatively recent phenomenon, agricultural co-operatives have a long history in Turkey, which is often traced back to the Ahi movement of the Ottoman era. The movement was committed to conduct commercial activities in an ethical way without exploiting either producers or consumers

(Okan and Okan, 2013, 8). Apart from the Ahi movement, the so-called country chests and Tariş (union of fig producers, which still exists today) are considered to be noteworthy early co-operative-like efforts in the pre-Turkish Republic era. The former is a fund established by the farmers dating back to 1863 and can be considered a type of proto-credit co-operative. The latter, Tariş, dates back to the early 20th century, when fig producers established an organization called the Aydın Fig Producers Company in 1915, following many of the basic principles of co-operatives. This initiative is often regarded as the actual start of the co-operative movement in Turkey (Okan and Okan, 2013, 10). Nevertheless, the real significant development of co-operatives in the country occurred with the establishment of the Turkish Republic in 1923, especially until 1938, under the leadership of Atatürk (the founder of the Republic), who himself was a co-operator (Okan and Okan, 2013, 11). Relatedly, Ballı (2020, 124) underlines that while there had been a number of legal arrangements on agricultural co-operatives earlier, 1935 was a turning point for the development of the legal framework of co-operativism in Turkey, as two major laws, namely, the Law on Agriculture Sales Co-operatives and Unions (No. 2834) and the Law on Agriculture Credit Co-operatives (No. 2836), were enacted.

The suitable legal, institutional, and social environment in the early years of the Republic paved the way for the proliferation of co-operatives in Turkey. Article 51 of the 1961 Constitution, which reads "the state takes the necessary precautions that will enable development of co-operatives," required active involvement of the state in co-operative efforts (Ministry of Customs and Trade, 2021). This meant that co-operatives became a part of the national plans, given that Turkey adopted a planned approach to development, steered by government-driven five-year development plans, starting from the early 1960s. Although almost all five-year development plans of these years were committed to encourage and support co-operatives, the second five-year development plan (1968–1972) gave particular emphasis to them. The common motto of the following plans was supporting "strong, effective, and democratic co-operatives based on voluntary initiatives," whilst in the seventh plan (1996–2000), "the thrust turned to the establishment and development of apex organizations in the form of co-operative unions" (Okan and Okan, 2013, 13).

At the same time, the regulatory framework for co-operatives has changed several times with important organizational and functional implications. With regard to agricultural sales co-operatives, for example, from the mid-1930s, when they were established to support their members through "facilitating the marketing of their crops, ensuring fair prices, processing and marketing their produce, ensuring crop standardization to increase exports, provision of cheap agricultural tools, machinery and inputs," until the mid-1980s, they had "relatively democratic and participatory structures" (Aydın, 2010, 162). However, from the mid-1980s onwards, this would change with interventions in the legal framework which significantly reduced the autonomy of these co-operatives, turning them into 'parastatal institutions' (Aydın, 2010, 162). Ballı (2020, 127) states that these interventions were a manifestation of the rise of economic liberalism in the 1980s. While the emphasis on state support for the development of co-operatives continued in the 1982 Constitution, Ballı points out that there has been at the same time a significant state grip over co-operatives (Ballı, 2020, 128). After 2001, with ARIP, the regulation of agricultural sales co-operatives underwent yet another set of changes, further eroding the already crucially limited capacity they had to support their members by a paradoxical mix of privatization while simultaneously increasing state control over their administrative framework (Aydın, 2010).

Currently, there are 84,232 co-operatives with 8,109,225 members in Turkey. The 26 different co-operative types fall under the mandate of one of the three key responsible ministries according to their main sector of activity (the Ministry of Customs and Trade; the Ministry of Food, Agriculture, and Livestock; and the Ministry of Environment and Urbanization) (Ministry of Customs and Trade, 2021). Of these different types of co-operatives, the Ministry of Customs and Trade regulates the most. Importantly, retail and consumer co-ops, including agricultural sales co-ops and other consumer co-ops specializing in food and related products, are under the jurisdiction of this ministry. The Ministry of Food, Agriculture, and Livestock, on the other hand, regulates all other co-operatives related to agriculture, the largest types being agricultural development, agricultural credit, and irrigation co-ops (Duguid et al., 2015).

The current system in place detailing the types of co-operatives in Turkey is rather complex. Agricultural Development Co-operatives (ADCs) usually have a specific focus such as olive, dairy, or fruit production, although they may diversify their activities in time. Irrigation, fisheries, and sugar beet co-operatives, on the other hand, provide a range of services with the ultimate goal of improving the socio-economic status of their members, much like the agricultural development co-operatives. There are two other types of co-operatives that are also operating in the agricultural sector, namely, agricultural credit co-operatives and agricultural sales co-operatives. We also see that co-operatives in Turkey are encouraged to integrate both vertically and horizontally, in which case they are provided with tax exemptions (Duguid et al., 2015, 106; Okan and Okan, 2013, 38). Specifically, Law No. 1163 allows a three-tier system in this respect: primary co-operatives, unions, and central unions. Notably, four unions of agricultural sales co-operatives are amongst the 500 largest businesses in Turkey, namely, Trakyabirlik, Marmarabirlik, Tariş Üzüm Birliği, and Tariş Pamuk Birliği. Involvement in politics, especially for the heads of unions, is not rare. Members, as a result, "stigmatize the managers of apex organizations as 'political ladder climbers' or 'ego builders,' which inevitably results in lack of support to the unions" (Okan and Okan, 2013, 39). The National Co-operative Strategy and Action Plan (2012–2016), on the other hand, cites 'poor management/governance,' 'lack of training and awareness,' and 'weak financial status' as the main reasons for poor performance of co-operatives in Turkey, the emphasis here on capable management of co-operatives paralleling some earlier findings in the literature (e.g. Abell, 1990).

The example of the Union of Hazelnut Sales Co-operatives (Fiskobirlik), which was founded in 1938, can provide crucial insights to the multifaceted problems that co-operatives are embedded in. Gürel et al. (2022, 107) state that "on the one hand, it [Fiskobirlik] represents all hazelnut producers and collects membership fees from them. On the other hand, it has acted as a government institution in regulating the hazelnut market." Ballı notes that throughout the 1940s and 1950s, Fiskobirlik maintained a relatively autonomous structure and played a central role in supporting small-scale hazelnut producers in the midst of economic challenges during the Second World War and its aftermath, through an emphasis on improving production conditions, providing inputs to villagers at favourable prices, and increasing export opportunities (Ballı, 2020, 138–140). This relative autonomy, however, would significantly diminish in the 1960s. "From the mid-1960s to the mid-2000s, Fiskobirlik purchased hazelnuts from its member co-operatives on behalf of the government treasury at pre-determined prices. . . . Historically, political concerns have been important in price determinations" (Gürel et al., 2022, 107). In the early 2000s, with the restructuring of unions arguably to make them autonomous, actual implication has been rendering Fiskobirlik dysfunctional in the context of harsh competition in the hazelnut market (Ballı, 2020, 145). In this regard, Kaynar notes that with Fiskobirlik not able to address their needs, some hazelnut producer villages have been establishing agricultural development co-operatives in order to sustain their livelihoods and continue hazelnut production (Kaynar, 2021, 142).

Given that around 85% of farmers in Turkey are considered small-scale, about two-thirds of agricultural establishments operating in less than five hectares of land (Adaman, 2021, 17; Kaya, 2019, 1438), co-operatives are seen as shields for small farmers against larger firms and powerful intermediaries. According to Aysu (2019, 88–89), agricultural development co-operatives in particular are essential in this context of small farmer-dominated agriculture because these farmers produce multiple crops and engage in animal husbandry as well, rather than a single produce. For this model of production, Aysu notes, agricultural development co-operatives can serve multiple functions that can address farmers' diverse needs (Aysu, 2019, 89). It has also been underlined that co-operatives aim to improve regional and national development by focusing on some key dimensions of development such as ecological sensitivity as well as women's empowerment and participation (Barut, 2017, 120). In the end, Turkey has a large co-operative sector; hence, "the domain of good and bad, successful and failed, small and large co-operatives is substantial" (Okan and Okan, 2013, 61). There is obviously a need to study examples of Turkish co-operatives in detail if we are to solve this mystery as to how and why, in the very same environment, some co-ops are successful whereas others are not, perhaps with a fresh definition of 'success,' to which we hope to contribute in this book.

A relevant point emphasized in studies focusing on agricultural co-operatives in Turkey is that traditional agricultural co-operative structures have rather limited potential to offer an alternative to the existing producer–consumer relations. Şahin (2020, 93–94), for example, argues that traditional co-operatives, including those operating in agricultural development, often lack democratic organizational mechanisms such as equal voting, they are more inclined towards operations of a firm prioritizing profit-making in competitive markets, and they usually focus on benefits to producers without a concern for agricultural workers, gender inequalities, or consumers. More recently, there are some agricultural co-operatives which have managed to divert from this more traditional model, such as Tire Milk Producers Development Co-operative, Hopa Tea Co-operative, Özçay Co-operative, and Ovacık Agricultural Development Co-operative, amongst others (Şahin, 2020). These examples exhibit, albeit in different forms, mechanisms that aim to contribute to the well-being of their members, without, to the extent possible, mimicking for-profit firm structures and operations. Some of these mechanisms include close relations with consumer co-operatives (e.g. Hopa co-op), establishment of health facilities or spaces for regenerating social relations (e.g. Tire and Hopa co-ops), developing ties with local administrations for community development (e.g. Ovacık co-op itself was facilitated by Ovacık Municipality), and prioritizing participation of women in the co-op labour (e.g. Ovacık co-op) (Şahin, 2020). In the case of the Tire co-op, its co-operation with İzmir Municipality since 2008, based on horizontal organizational collaboration, has been an important factor in overcoming problems of producer dependency on big companies operating in the milk market (Yıldırım, 2020, 48). Thereby, there is an increasing development of novel approaches, 'new generation' co-operatives, which aim to address the problematic organizational features of the traditional co-operatives, while at the same time struggling to find space in the transformed landscape of neo-liberalized agriculture and rural–urban relations. An important debate, therefore, is how to think of an alternative pathway that producer co-operatives and consumer co-operatives can together form, which speaks to the challenges we identified earlier with regard to AFNs' potential to provide a genuine alternative to the dominant food system. The in-depth analysis of BÜKOOP as a consumer co-op and Vakıflı co-op as a women's producer co-op aims to unfold both the opportunities and constraints towards building of this alternative.

A final note in this section concerns the roles played by women's co-ops in Turkey. Although official government data are not disaggregated by gender, we know that in agricultural co-operatives, the ratio of women in total membership is very low (Okan and Okan, 2013, 41); in fact, most agricultural co-operatives have almost exclusively men as members (Duguid et al., 2015, 35). Women are also less likely to be in leadership positions within mixed (male and female members) co-operatives. Women's engagement with co-operatives is limited by gender inequalities in literacy levels, low business skills, lack of land ownership, and limited access to credit and information. Women's role, however, began to increase in recent decades, especially since the establishment of first women's co-operatives in 1999. According to a survey, 67% of active women co-operatives are found to be enterprise co-operatives, 29% are agricultural co-operatives, and the remaining operate in small arts, consumers, and manufacturing (Duguid et al., 2015). We see that several government bodies are involved in actively supporting women's co-operatives, including the Ministry of Commerce and Trade (through tax exemptions and low-interest long-term credits) and the Ministry of Education (through vocational training towards women) (Okan and Okan, 2013, 42; Özdemir, 2013, 302). The support of the state, however, is seen as unsystematic and unpredictable, often depending on political loyalty (Çınar et al., 2021, 787).

The literature on women's co-operatives highlights their key economic and non-economic benefits. A recent study on women's co-operatives in Turkey (Çınar et al., 2021) found that women could indeed make considerable economic gains as well as reaping psychological, social, and organizational benefits as participants of women's co-operatives. Accordingly, women co-operators could build stronger bonds with other co-op members, finding opportunities to establish connections with women from different classes or ethnic backgrounds. Likely contributions of key individuals and 'pioneer women' (Dalkıran, 2017, 10) might also be noteworthy in this regard, as the example of a women's co-operative in Seferihisar (close to Izmir in the Aegean region), for which the district mayor's wife played a key role as the founding president of the women's co-operative in the district, illustrates (Barut, 2017, 126). A World Bank report on women's co-operatives in Turkey (Duguid et al., 2015) also asserts that women's co-operatives are of prime importance since they provide jobs and a social outlet for women. Accordingly, the income earned as a result of co-op activities not only is important for their households but also improves their self-esteem. Specifically, Duguid et al. (2015, 45) find that the number one reason for the establishment of 59% of active co-operatives they studied is 'providing jobs for women,' followed by 'empowering women socially' (17%) and 'finding solutions to women's issues' (16%) (Duguid et al., 2015, 45). This clear emphasis on economic benefits of co-ops for women is in line with the findings in the relevant literature in the rest of the world (Jones et al., 2012, 20–24).

Still, the benefits associated with women's co-operatives are not limited to economic ones and also include a diverse set of psychological and social achievements. Women's empowerment via co-operatives include higher self-confidence, better critical thinking and decision making, enhanced vision of future, mobility, and visibility, heightened decision making in the household, improved status in social circles, ability to interact effectively in the public sphere, and participation and solidarity in non-family groups.

(Çınar et al., 2021, 797)

Besides, women's co-operatives may foster women's ability to negotiate with, say, potential customers and/or government bodies. This and other skills, as well as valuable information regarding new resources and markets, spill over to all involved co-operators. Women's co-operatives in Turkey, however, face challenges in areas related to finance and legislation. Additional concerns include lack of integration between different co-operatives and low skills in governing a co-operative (Duguid et al., 2015; Özdemir, 2013). Another dimension is that the benefits women get from co-ops may vary in relative terms, even within the same co-operative for different members depending on their pre-existing conditions (Çınar et al., 2021, 792–793), with obvious links to class differences. Overall, it is possible to conclude that AFNs in general and co-operatives in particular may assume important roles with regard to women's empowerment by enabling economic independence, psychological gains, and social solidarity for their members.

Methodologically, in this study, we follow a multi-source strategy for both co-ops, involving in-depth interviews with founders, members, volunteers, and producers/consumers as well as a thorough analysis of archival and organizational documents. Additional data are derived from the co-op web pages, press reports and bulletins, and other relevant documents (e.g. social media accounts). The fact that we are amongst the founders of the co-op analysed in the first case study enables us to incorporate, when relevant, our own experiences as well, in line with the premises of analytic auto-ethnography (Anderson, 2006). (For detailed discussions regarding auto-ethnography, see Anderson, 2006; Denshire, 2014; Ellis et al., 2011; Wall, 2008; and the 2006 special issue of *Journal of Contemporary Ethnography*). The methodology for the second case study is similar and involves in-depth interviews with the producers of the Vakıflı co-op, in addition to a thorough analysis of the available secondary sources (e.g. archival research, web page of the co-op, and press coverage). We benefit from auto-ethnographic evidence in this case study as well, given our experience of working together with the Vakıflı co-op since the foundation of BÜKOOP. In fact, for a couple of years, one of us was responsible from the first key product BÜKOOP procured from Vakıflı, pomegranate syrup.

As a final note in this chapter, we would like to state that we have been working on BÜKOOP since its foundation, and this research has already produced an article (see Öz and Aksoy, 2019). For the present study, we have revised and updated this earlier research we conducted on BÜKOOP, which has been facing significant external pressures and challenges since then, including but not limited to the impact of the pandemic. The Vakıflı co-op, on the other hand, has challenges of its own, coupled with those associated with the general state of agriculture in the country and migration to urban areas. On top of these came a heavy nation-wide economic crisis, the civil war in Syria, the pandemic, and, most recently, three powerful earthquakes which struck that part of the country in February 2023, the third one hitting Vakıflı particularly hard. There were no casualties in Vakıflı, but the quakes left the village's stone houses heavily damaged, and the 130 villagers have been forced to live in tents.

References

Abell, P. (1990). Supporting industrial co-operatives in developing countries: Some Tanzanian experiences. *Economic and Industrial Democracy*, 11(4), 483–504. https://doi.org/10.1177/0143831X9001100403

Adaman, F. (2021). *Sürdürülebilir ve Dirençli Bir Gıda Sistemi: Türkiye Analizi.* İstanbul Politikalar Merkezi.

Adaman, F., & Akbulut, B. (2016). Alternatif ekonomiler üzerine bir ufuk turu. *Birikim*, January, 31–38.

Ajates Gonzales, R. (2017). Going back to go forwards? From multi-stakeholder cooperatives to open cooperatives in food and farming. *Journal of Rural Studies*, 53, 278–290. https://doi.org/10.1016/j.jrurstud.2017.02.018

Ajates, R. (2021). Reducing the risk of co-optation in alternative food networks: Multistakeholder co-operatives, social capital, and third spaces of co-operation. *Sustainability*, 13, 11219. https://doi.org/10.3390/su132011219

Allen, P., Fitzsimmons, M., Goodman, M., & Warner, K. (2003). Shifting plates in the agri-food landscape: The tectonics of alternative agri-food initiatives in California. *Journal of Rural Studies*, 19, 61–75. https://doi.org/10.1016/S0743-0167(02)00047-5

Anderson, C. R., Brushett, L., Gray, T., & Renting, H. (2014). Working together to build co-operative food systems. *Journal of Agriculture, Food Systems, and Community Development*, 4(3), 3–9. https://doi.org/10.5304/jafscd.2014.043.017

Anderson, L. (2006). Analytic auto-ethnography. *Journal of Contemporary Ethnography*, 35(4), 373–395. https://doi.org/10.1177/0891241605280449

Ashforth, B. E., & Reingen, P. H. (2014). Functions of dysfunction: Managing the dynamics of an organizational duality in a natural food cooperative. *Administrative Science Quarterly*, 59(3), 474–516. https://doi.org/10.1177/0001839214537811

Atasoy, Y. (2013). Supermarket expansion in Turkey: Shifting relations of food provisioning. *Journal of Agrarian Change*, 13(4), 547–570. https://doi.org/10.1111/j.1471-0366.2012.00382.x

Aydın, Z. (2010). Neo-liberal transformation of Turkish agriculture. *Journal of Agrarian Change*, 10(2), 149–187. https://doi.org/10.1111/j.1471-0366.2009.00241.x

Aysu, A. (2019). *Kooperatifler*. Yeni İnsan Yayınevi.

Ballı, E. (2020). Türkiye'de tarımsal kooperatifçiliğin gelişimi ve Fiskobirlik: Tarihsel bir değerlendirme. In F. S. Öngel & U. D. Yıldırım (eds.) *Krize Karşı Kooperatifler: Deneyimler, Tartışmalar, Alternatifler* (pp. 117–152). NotaBene Yayınları.

Barut, Y. (2017). Women's co-operatives' contributions to local region economy: Sefer-ihisar Agricultural Co-operative Development Model – Turkey. *Management Studies*, 5(2), 120–127. https://doi.org/10.17265/2328-2185/2017.02.004

Bellante, L. (2017). Building the local food movement in Chiapas, Mexico: Rationales, benefits and limitations. *Agriculture and Human Values*, 34, 119–134. https://doi.org/10.1007/s10460-016-9700-9

Bijman, J., & Wijers, G. (2019). Exploring the inclusiveness of producer cooperatives. *Current Opinion in Environmental Sustainability*, 41, 74–79. https://doi.org/10.1016/j.cosust.2019.11.005

Chen, K. K. (2016). Plan your burn, burn your plan: How decentralization, storytelling, and communification can support participatory practices. *The Sociological Quarterly*, 57, 71–97. https://doi.org/10.1111/tsq.12115

Çınar, K., Akyüz, S., Uğur-Çınar, M., & Öncüler-Yayalar, E. (2021). Faces and phases of women's empowerment: The case of women's co-operatives in Turkey. *Social Politics*, 28(3), 778–805. https://doi.org/10.1093/sp/jxz032

Clapp, J. (2022). The rise of big food and agriculture: Corporate influence in the food system. In C. Sage (ed.) *A Research Agenda for Food Systems* (pp. 45–66). Edward Elgar Publishing.

Dalkıran, G. B. (2017). The support of women's work within co-operative enterprises: Sample of Turkey. *Social Sciences Research Journal*, 6(3), 1–11.

Daya, S., & Authar, R. (2012). Self, others and objects in an 'alternative economy': Personal narratives from the Heiveld Rooibos Co-operative. *Geoforum*, 43, 885–893. https://doi.org/10.1016/j.geoforum.2012.03.017

Demirkılıç, S., Özertan, G., & Tekgüç, H. (2022). The evolution of unprocessed food inflation in Turkey: An exploratory study on select products. *New Perspectives on Turkey*, 67, 57–82. https://doi.org/10.1017/npt.2022.9

Denshire, S. (2014). On auto-ethnography. *Current Sociology Review*, 62(6), 831–850. https://doi.org/10.1177/0011392114533339

Duguid, F., Durutaş, G., & Wodzicki, M. (2015). *The Current State of Women's Co-operatives in Turkey*. The World Bank.

Duncan, J., & Pascucci, S. (2017). Mapping the organisational forms of networks of alternative food networks: Implications for transition. *Sociologia Ruralis*, 57(3), 316–339. https://doi.org/10.1111/soru.12167

DuPuis, E. M., & Goodman, D. (2005). Should we go 'home' to eat? Toward a reflexive politics of localism. *Journal of Rural Studies*, 21(3), 359–371. https://doi.org/10.1016/j.jrurstud.2005.05.011

Ellis, C., Adams, T. E., & Bochner, A. P. (2011). Autoethnography: An overview. *Historical Social Research*, 36(4), 273–290. www.jstor.org/stable/23032294

FAO, IFAD, UNICEF, WFP, & WHO. (2021). *The State of Food Security and Nutrition in the World 2021: Transforming Food Systems for Food Security, Improved Nutrition and Affordable Healthy Diets for All*. FAO. https://doi.org/10.4060/cb4474en

Feenstra, G. W. (1997). Local food systems and sustainable communities. *American Journal of Alternative Agriculture*, 12(1), 28–36. https://doi.org/10.1017/S0889189300007165

Friedmann, H. (1995). Food politics: New dangers, new possibilities. In P. McMichael (ed.) *Food and Agrarian Orders in the World Economy* (pp. 15–33). Praeger Publishing.

Forssell, S., & Lankoski, L. (2015). The sustainability promise of alternative food networks: An examination through 'alternative' characteristics. *Agriculture and Human Values*, 32, 63–75. https://doi.org/10.1007/s10460-014-9516-4

Fournier, V. (2008). Escaping from the economy: The politics of degrowth. *International Journal of Sociology and Social Policy*, 28(11/12), 528–545. https://doi.org/10.1108/01443330810915233

Freidberg, S. E., & Goldstein, L. (2011). Alternative food in the Global South: Reflections on a direct marketing initiative in Kenya. *Journal of Rural Studies*, 27(1), 24–34. https://doi.org/10.1016/j.jrurstud.2010.07.003

Gibson-Graham, J. K. (2003). Enabling ethical economies: Cooperativism and class. *Critical Sociology*, 29(2), 123–161. https://doi.org/10.1163/156916303769155788

Gibson-Graham, J. K. (2008). Diverse economies: Performative practices for 'other worlds'. *Progress in Human Geography*, 32(5), 613–632. https://doi.org/10.1177/0309132508090821

Gonzales, V., & Philips, R. G. (2013). Linking past, present and future: An introduction to co-operatives and community development. In V. Gonzales & R. G. Philips (eds.) *Cooperatives and Community Development* (pp. 1–21). Routledge.

Goodman, D., Dupuis, E. M., & Goodman, M. K. (2012). *Alternative Food Networks: Knowledge, Practice and Politics*. Routledge.

Gray, T. W. (2014). Historical tensions, institutionalization, and the need for multistakeholder co-operatives [Commentary]. *Journal of Agriculture, Food Systems, and Community Development*, 4(3), 23–28. https://doi.org/10.5304/jafscd.2014.043.013

Gritzas, G., & Kavoulakos, K. I. (2016). Diverse economies and alternative spaces: An overview of approaches and practices. *European Urban and Regional Studies*, 23(4), 917–934. https://doi.org/10.1177/0969776415573778

Gürel, B., Küçük, B., & Taş, S. (2022). The rural roots of the rise of the Justice and Development Party in Turkey. In I. Scoones, M. Edelman, S. M. Borras, L. F. Forrero, R. Hall, W. Wolford, & B. White (eds.) *Authoritarian Populism and the Rural World* (pp. 97–119). Routledge.

Guthman, J. (2008). Neoliberalism and the making of food politics in California. *Geoforum*, 39, 1171–1183. https://doi.org/10.1016/j.geoforum.2006.09.002

Haedicke, M. A. (2012). Keeping our mission, changing our system: Translation and organisational change in natural food co-ops. *The Sociological Quarterly*, 53(1), 44–67. https://doi.org/10.1111/j.1533-8525.2011.01225.x

Hergesheimer, C., & Wittman, H. (2012). Weaving chains of grain: Social histories and emerging grain initiatives in SW British Columbia. *Food, Culture and Society*, 15(3), 375–393. https://doi.org/10.2752/175174412X13276629245803

Hibbert, S., Piacentini, M., & Al Dajani, H. (2003). Understanding volunteer motivation for participation in a community-based food co-operative. *International Journal of Nonprofit and Voluntary Sector Marketing*, 8(1), 30–42. https://doi.org/10.1002/nvsm.199

ICA. (2022). *What is a Co-operative?* www.ica.coop/en/cooperatives/what-is-a-cooperative (accessed on 16 November 2022).

ILO & ICA. (2014). *Co-operatives and the Sustainable Development Goals: A Contribution to the Post-2015 Development Debate*. ILO and ICA.

Ince, A., & Kadirbeyoğlu, Z. (2020). The politics of food: Commoning practices in alternative food networks in Istanbul. In D. Özkan & G. B. Büyüksaraç (eds.) *Commoning the City: Empirical Perspectives on Urban Ecology, Economics and Ethics* (pp. 37–50). Routledge.

IPES-Food (International Panel of Experts on Sustainable Food Systems). (2020). *COVID-19 and the Crisis in Food Systems: Symptoms, Causes, and Potential Solutions*. Communiqué by IPES-Food, April 2020. www.ipes-food.org/pages/covid19 (accessed on 6 July 2023).

Jarosz, L. (2008). The city in the country: Growing alternative food networks in Metropolitan areas. *Journal of Rural Studies*, 24(3), 231–244. https://doi.org/10.1016/j.jrurstud.2007.10.002

Jones, E., Smith, S., & Will, C. (2012). Women producers and the benefits of collective forms of enterprise. *Gender & Development*, 20(1), 13–32. https://doi.org/10.1080/13552074.2012.663640

Kadıköy Kooperatifi Kolektifi. (2020). Kadıköy kooperatifi deneyimi. In F. S. Öngel & U. D. Yıldırım (eds.) *Krize Karşı Kooperatifler: Deneyimler, Tartışmalar, Alternatifler* (pp. 153–182). NotaBene Yayınları.

Kadirbeyoğlu, Z., & Konya, N. (2017). Alternative food initiatives in Turkey. In F. Adaman, B. Akbulut, & M. Arsel (eds.) *Neoliberal Turkey and Its Discontents* (pp. 207–230). IB Taurus.

Kallis, G., Kerschner, C., & Martinez-Alier, J. (2012). The economics of de-growth. *Ecological Economics*, 84, 172–180. https://doi.org/10.1016/j.ecolecon.2012.08.017

Kaya, Ç. (2019). Sosyal iş modelleri ve sosyal girişimcilik: Boğaziçi Üniversitesi Tüketim Kooperatifi Örneği. *İşletme Araştırmaları Dergisi*, 11(3), 1433–1449.

Kaynar, İ. S. (2021). Fındık Üretiminde Sınıf İlişkilerinin ve Piyasanın Değişen Dinamikleri. In C. E. Şahin (eds.) *21. Yüzyıl Türkiye'sinde Tarım ve Kooperatifler* (pp. 115–147). NotaBene Yayınları.

Kopczyńska, E. (2017). Economies of acquaintances: Social relations during shopping at food markets and in consumers' food cooperatives. *East European Politics and Societies and Cultures*, 20(10), 1–22. https://doi.org/10.1177/0888325417710079

Lamine, C., Darolt, M., & Brandenburg, A. (2012). The civic and social dimensions of food production and distribution in alternative food networks in France and Southern Brazil. *International Journal of Sociology of Agriculture and Food*, 19(3), 383–401.

Leach, D. K. (2016). When freedom is not an endless meeting: A new look at efficiency in consensus-based decision making. *The Sociological Quarterly*, 57, 36–70. https://doi.org/10.1111/tsq.12137

Little, R., Maye, D., & Ilbery, B. (2010). Collective purchase: Moving local and organic foods beyond the niche market. *Environment and Planning A*, 42, 1797–1813. https://doi.org/10.1068/a4262

Lund, M. (2012). Multi-stakeholder co-operatives: Engines of innovation for building a healthier local food system and a healthier economy. *Journal of Co-operative Studies*, 45(1), 32–45.

Majee, W., & Hoyt, A. (2011). Co-operatives and community development: A perspective on the use of co-operatives in development. *Journal of Community Practice*, 19(1), 48–61. https://doi.org/10.1080/10705422.2011.550260

Mansbridge, J. J. (1979). The agony of inequality. In J. Case & R. C. R. Taylor (eds.) *Co-ops, Communes & Collectives: Experiments in Social Change* (pp. 194–205). Pantheon Books.

Mares, T. M., & Alkon, A. H. (2011). Mapping the food movement: Addressing inequality and neoliberalism. *Environment and Society: Advances in Research*, 2, 68–86. https://doi.org/10.3167/ares.2011.020105

Marsden, T., & Smith, E. (2005). Ecological entrepreneurship: Sustainable development in local communities through quality food production and local branding. *Geoforum*, 36(4), 440–451. https://doi.org/10.1016/j.geoforum.2004.07.008

Meliá-Marti, E., Tormo-Carbó, G., & Juliá-Igual, J. F. (2020). Does gender diversity affect performance in agri-food cooperatives? A moderated model. *Sustainability*, 12, 1–27.

Ministry of Customs and Trade (2021). *Türkiye'de Kooperatifçilik.* https://ticaret.gov. tr/kooperatifcilik/bilgi-bankasi/kooperatifler-hakkinda/turkiyede-kooperatifcilik (accessed on 4 February 2023).

Moon, S. (2022). Women's food work, food citizenship, & transnational consumer capitalism: A case study of a feminist food cooperative in South Korea. *Food, Culture & Society,* 25(3), 449–467. https://doi.org/10.1080/15528014.2021.1892255

Mooney, P. H. (2004). Democratizing rural economy: Institutional friction, sustainable struggle and the cooperative movement. *Rural Sociology,* 69(1), 76–98. https://doi. org/10.1526/003601104322919919

Okan, N. D., & Okan, C. (2013). *An Overview of Cooperatives in Turkey.* FAO Regional Office for Europe and Central Asia, Policy Studies on Rural Transition No. 2013-3. FAO.

Öz, Ö., & Aksoy, Z. (2019). Challenges of building alternatives: The experience of a consumer food co-operative in Istanbul. *Food, Culture & Society,* 22(3), 299–315. https://doi.org/10.1080/15528014.2019.1596529

Öz, Ö., & Çalışkan, K. (2010). An alternative market organization: The case of cut flower exchange in Turkey. *METU Studies in Development,* 37(2), 153–170. www2. feas.metu.edu.tr/metusd/ojs/index.php/metusd/article/view/287

Özdemir, G. (2013). Women's co-operatives in Turkey. *Procedia – Social and Behavioural Sciences,* 81, 300–305. https://doi.org/10.1016/j.sbspro.2013.06.432

Paranque, B., & Willmott, H. (2014). Cooperatives – saviours or gravediggers of capitalism? Critical performativity and the John Lewis Partnership. *Organization,* 21(5), 604–625. https://doi.org/10.1177/1350508414537622

Parkins, W., & Craig, G. (2009). Culture and the politics of alternative food networks. *Food, Culture & Society,* 12(1), 77–103. https://doi.org/10.2752/155280109X368679

Qazi, J. A., & Selfa, T. L. (2005). The politics of building alternative agro-food networks in the belly of agro-industry. *Food, Culture & Society,* 8(1), 45–72. https://doi. org/10.2752/155280105778055416

Renting, H., Marsden, T. K., & Banks, J. (2003). Understanding alternative food networks: Exploring the role of short food supply chains in rural development. *Environment and Planning A,* 35(3), 393–411.

Reyes, J. C., & Harnecker, C. P. (2013). An introduction to co-operatives. In C. P. Harnecker (ed.) *Co-operatives and Socialism: A View from Cuba* (pp. 25–45). Palgrave MacMillan.

Ribeiro, A. P., Harmsen, R., Feola, G., Carréon, J. R., & Worrell, E. (2021). Organising alternative food networks (AFNs): Challenges and facilitating conditions of different AFN types in three EU countries. *Sociologia Ruralis,* 61(2), 491–517. https://doi. org/10.1111/soru.12331

Rosol, M. (2020). On the significance of alternative economic practices: Reconceptualizing alterity in alternative food networks. *Economic Geography,* 96(1), 52–76. https://doi.org/10.1080/00130095.2019.1701430

Rothschild-Whitt, J. (1979). Conditions for democracy: Making organizations work. In J. Case & R. J. R. Taylor (eds.) *Co-ops, Communes & Collectives: Experiments in Social Change* (pp. 215–244). Pantheon Books.

Rothschild-Whitt, J., & Whitt, J. A. (1986). Worker-owners as an emergent class: Effects of co-operative work on job satisfaction, alienation, and stress. *Economic and Industrial Democracy,* 7, 297–317. https://doi.org/10.1177/0143831X8673004

Şahin, Ç. E. (2020). Türkiye tarımının güncel sorunlarının çözümününde kooperatifler bir model olabilir mi? Fırsatlar ve handikaplar üzerine düşünceler. In F. S. Öngel & U. D. Yıldırım (eds.) *Krize Karşı Kooperatifler: Deneyimler, Tartışmalar, Alternatifler* (pp. 79–115). NotaBene Yayınları.

Sarmiento, E. R. (2017). Synergies in alternative food network research: Embodiment, diverse economies, and more-than-human food geographies. *Agriculture and Human Values*, 34, 485–497. https://doi.org/10.1007/s10460-016-9753-9

Sato, C., & Soto Alarcón, J. M. (2019). Toward a post-capitalist feminist political ecology's approach to the commons and commoning. *International Journal of the Commons*, 13(1), 36–61.

Schneider, F., Giorgios, K., & Martinez-Alier, J. (2010). Crisis or opportunity? Economic de-growth for social equity and ecological sustainability. Introduction to this special issue. *Journal of Cleaner Production*, 18, 511–518. https://doi.org/10.1016/j.jclepro.2010.01.014

Sharpe, S. (2014). Potentiality and impotentiality in J. K. Gibson-Graham. *Rethinking Marxism: A Journal of Economics, Culture & Society*, 26(1), 27–43. https://doi.org/10.1080/08935696.2014.857842

Si, Z., Schumilas, T., & Scott, S. (2015). Characterizing alternative food networks in China. *Agriculture and Human Values*, 32, 299–313. https://doi.org/10.1007/s10460-014-9530-6

Soysal Al, I. (2020). The promising momentum and collective practices of the recently expanding network of consumer-led ecological food initiatives in Turkey. *İstanbul Üniversitesi Sosyoloji Dergisi*, 40(1), 129–162. https://doi.org/10.26650/SJ.2020.40.1.0046

Stryjan, Y. (1994). Understanding co-operatives: The reproduction perspective. *Annals of Public and Co-operative Economics*, 65(1), 59–80.

Tregear, A. (2011). Progressing knowledge in alternative and local food networks: Critical reflections and a research agenda. *Journal of Rural Studies*, 27, 419–430. https://doi.org/10.1016/j.jrurstud.2011.06.003

Wall, S. (2008). Easier said than done: Writing an autoethnography. *International Journal of Qualitative Methods*, 7(1), 38–53. https://doi.org/10.1177/160940690800700103

Watts, D. C. H., Ilbery, B., & Maye, D. (2005). Making reconnections in agro-food geography: Alternative systems of food provision. *Progress in Human Geography*, 29(1), 22–40. https://doi.org/10.1191/0309132505ph526oa

Wertheim, E. G. (1976). Evolution of structure and process in voluntary organizations: A study of thirty-five consumer food cooperatives. *Journal of Voluntary Action Research*, 4–15. https://doi.org/10.1177/089976407600500102

Whatmore, S., & Thorne, L. (1997). Nourishing networks: Alternative geographies of food. In D. Goodman & M. J. Watts (eds.) *Globalising Food: Agrarian Questions and Global Restructuring* (pp. 287–304). Routledge.

Winter, M. (2003). Embeddedness, the new food economy and defensive localism. *Journal of Rural Studies*, 19(1), 23–32. https://doi.org/10.1016/S0743-0167(02)00053-0

World Bank. (2023). *Food Security Update - June 29, 2023.* worldbank.org (accessed on 12 July 2023).

Yıldırım, U. D. (2020). Belediyeler ve kooperatifler ekseninde Türkiye tarımında alternatif kamusallık deneyimleri: Olanaklar ve sınırlar. In F. S. Öngel & U. D. Yıldırım (eds.) *Krize Karşı Kooperatifler: Deneyimler, Tartışmalar, Alternatifler* (pp. 25–78). NotaBene Yayınları.

Zitcer, A. (2015). Food co-ops and the paradox of exclusivity. *Antipode*, 47(3), 812–828. https://doi.org/10.1111/anti.12129

2 The experience of a consumer food co-op
BÜKOOP

The history of BÜKOOP

BÜKOOP was officially established in 2009 by a group of volunteers who work at Boğaziçi University in Istanbul, as an alternative model for organizing economic activity. Boğaziçi is a public university (its origins go back to the Robert College of 1863) and has eight campuses in Istanbul with about 17,000 students and 1,250 academic and 1,400 administrative staff members. Boğaziçi recruits from the top 10 per cent of students in the national university entrance exams. Its 'strategic plan' states amongst its priorities 'being a green campus' and 'being sensitive to the environment,' and it hosts a number of relevant student clubs and university committees dedicated to protection of nature.

BÜKOOP, as a consumer food co-operative, aims at redefining the organization of producer and consumer relations in a way that it is possible to provide justice for farmers and consumers simultaneously. BÜKOOP defends the right to know and contributes towards shaping every step involved in the process, from the seed to the kitchen table. While doing so, the co-op is determined to maintain a flat organizational structure that facilitates participation and solidarity amongst members, volunteers, and supporters. Its mission, in other words, far exceeds bringing healthy food to the campus and extends to a transformative project that involves not only a redefinition of the relations with external constitutes but also that of internal organization.

Although BÜKOOP was legally established in 2009, the discussions and preparations for its foundation began one year earlier, in 2008. The dream was that a consumer food co-op, established at Boğaziçi University in co-operation with two unions – Eğitim-Sen representing the university employees and Çiftçi-Sen representing small farmers – could be a model that would inspire other university and perhaps neighbourhood co-ops. It was envisaged that all this in turn could have a real impact on farmers and consumers alike. These two unions played an important part in the early stages of BÜKOOP's foundation, and their role faded out gradually.

The rest of 2008 passed with intensive meetings, sometimes involving representatives/supporters from the farmers' side (Tohum Izi Association in

DOI: 10.4324/9781003289166-2

particular), to discuss the details of this dream. If the dream came true, a network of producer co-operatives would be in solidarity with a network of consumer co-operatives, blurring the dichotomy of producer versus consumer, and even rural versus urban. This co-operation would encourage and support an organized society, active participation, and solidarity on both ends, in line with Mooney's (2004) assertion of co-ops' ability to democratize both production and consumption spheres. Following a one-year preparation and securing a building space from the university administration, BÜKOOP was officially established in December 2009. The co-op began to work with an accountant/bookkeeper on a part-time basis since then, who is the only paid worker of the co-op to date. The co-op insists entire work be conducted by volunteers so that a 'co-op spirit' could be established and maintained, which also reflects Rosol's (2020, 59) point on working practices as one of the key dimensions of alternative economies.

Preparations intensified during the first quarter of 2010: The building space was turned into a co-op, first orders were planned, and the co-op started to accept members. The plan was to proceed at a slow pace initially: 'Slow co-op' was the motto. Accordingly, a pilot stage was designed. At this stage, only academic and administrative staff were allowed to be members; the co-op would work with a single producer co-operative (Kibele) and begin with a limited number of items including olives and olive oil, cheese, honey and jams, flour, rice, and beans. A web page was designed (www.bukoop.org); the co-op began accepting orders and distributed them to the members once a month. There were about 100 members at the end of the first year (i.e. 2010), and about half of them were regularly shopping from the co-op. With confidence gained from achieving the goals of the initial stage satisfactorily, BÜKOOP decided to enlarge its membership to the alumni and students. The co-op stopped taking orders and distributing them (this practice of pre-ordering is now only used for fresh milk) and instead began to rely on volunteers to keep the co-op open twice a day, around noon and in the evening.

The alumni were living across Istanbul, making it difficult for them to visit the co-op regularly. Demands from the alumni for online shopping and shipment were discussed and rejected by the co-op, which gives special emphasis to face-to-face contact to maintain the co-op spirit. A practice called 'Loooong Saturdays,' however, was introduced to cater to the demands of those who could not visit the co-op during weekdays. Moreover, the co-op organized meetings, workshops, and seminars with producers and farmers, and also arranged visits to the farms. This is of critical importance since it enables a mutual learning process and provides a genuine link between producers and the co-op members. One example for the producer co-ops that BÜKOOP works with since these initial stages is the Vakıflı co-op located on the Mediterranean coast of Turkey, a women's co-operative that produces hand-made jams and syrups, which will be analysed in detail in the next chapter.

BÜKOOP started to issue a newsletter and organize events/seminars and stands in different campuses of the university. As BÜKOOP's visibility increased, the number of members doubled and reached about 200, not only members but also about 600 university employees and students regularly shopping at the co-op. Likewise, the number of producers the co-op works with also increased (paying attention to the principle of working with organized and small farmers who avoid using chemicals and prefer to use local seeds), together with the number and range of products offered. This meant introducing more structure. A computer-based stock system was established, and each product was assigned to a particular volunteer, who assumed responsibility for everything about this product, ranging from relations with the farmer to organizing packaging and pricing. More formal procedures for evaluating and deciding about whether or not the co-op would sell a new product were established, echoing Wertheim's (1976) second stage of organizational development. Each product sold at the co-op now has a 'product information form,' also feeding a process of demystification with regard to information, hence working against consolidation of power (Rothschild-Whitt, 1979). The 'product information form' is very detailed and involves questions on the specifics of the production process (e.g. how the product is produced, the kind of seeds used, and whether or not pesticides are used) and the producer (e.g., size, the number of employees, and working conditions).

It is necessary to state at this juncture that BÜKOOP does not require an organic certification from producers. For producers, the associated bureaucratic procedures might be hard to deal with and the burden of certification costs – in euros, which is of particular concern given the considerable devaluation of Turkish lira in recent years – might be heavy. The organic certificate is also problematized since, if a farmer does not have an organic certificate, this does not mean s/he is not engaging in ecological farming. Besides, the process itself might be "impersonal and alienating to the farmer and does not involve the customer at all," and "as such, it undermines some of the principles AFNs are built upon" (Türkkan, 2020, 30). In fact, as suggested in the literature, many other actors in alternative food networks (AFNs) "claim to empower small-scale farming and local food chains without requiring organic certification" (Soysal Al and Küçük, 2019, 174). Instead, AFNs "offer alternatives through certain principles and values such as respect for ecology, small farming, sustainable agriculture, and healthy food. They mostly assert that the global commoditisation of food has also led to urban/rural distancing and to our loss of both control of the land and knowledge of small farming" (Soysal Al and Küçük, 2019, 174). This is also relevant for the discussion presented in Chapter 1 about the differences between AFNs in the North, where organic certification is a key feature, and the South, where alternative certification mechanisms such as 'participatory guarantee systems' (PGS) are important.

This does not, however, mean that farmers and their products are not carefully scrutinized. As mentioned earlier, in BÜKOOP the 'product information form' details whether the producer engages in ecological farming, adopts local agroecological techniques, uses local seeds, and provides a just working environment in case they have employees. BÜKOOP finds potential producers by the help of the Farmers' Union and other food co-operatives/communities. This close link with the union and other food co-ops also works as a crucial component of monitoring after BÜKOOP starts to work with these producers, in a context where the union and the farmers engaging in agroecological production and co-ops who buy food from them are in regular and close contact which enables mutual learning and information exchange.

The process of finding and initiating relations with producers may take a considerable time for BÜKOOP, although there are exceptions. A relatively recent addition to BÜKOOP's list of producers, the Gödence co-operative near Izmir in the Aegean region, for example, took place very quickly in relative terms given that the general approach to the food system and the basic principles of BÜKOOP and Gödence are quite similar. Hence, it did not take long for Gödence and BÜKOOP to start working together, and both sides were rather surprised that they could not 'find' each other earlier. They nevertheless did in the end, confirming the view that the paths of like-minded people will cross sooner or later. The case of the Gödence co-operative is also of particular relevance for the purposes of this study since it provides a successful example of how an old-wave co-op (established in 1972) can transform itself successfully, maintaining its original goals and ideals, particularly with regard to its commitment to establish a 'solid bridge between producers and consumers.'

Potential producers themselves might also approach BÜKOOP, in which case they are asked to fill the 'product information form' as a first step. The details in the filled-in form are then discussed by the volunteers, and a visit to the farm is organized if necessary. A direct, trust-based, and long-term relationship is established and maintained with the chosen producers that conform to the established criteria of BÜKOOP. Even though this process is principally in line with PGS, there is not yet a systematized PGS certification scheme, but the aim is to learn from the PGS experiences around the world and adopt it in the long term.

It is very rare that this trust-based relationship ends once it starts. If it does, it is usually related to such reasons as the producers deciding to end their activities due to personal/economic rationales. One such case, for instance, took place in summer 2022 when the producer from which BÜKOOP used to procure eggs ended production since one of the two brothers running the farm went abroad and the other found another job, underlining, amongst other things, that small-scale production of eggs is a real challenge. More generally, life for many small producers has indeed become hard in recent years, since they have been first hit by the pandemic; then a heavy, country-wide economic crisis; and most recently a set of catastrophic earthquakes. BÜKOOP too has had to face these crises and their severe consequences.

When Turkey reported its first COVID-19 case on 11 March 2020, one of us (Özlem) was a volunteer at the co-op and remembers that the co-op witnessed a very good volume of sales on that day, together with the anxiety in the eyes of those rushing to buy supplies, not knowing when again they could have access to such food that they can trust. "Let me buy my last kg of healthy oranges, who knows when I'll be able to come again," one buyer explained the reason for her rush. Before the lockdowns started later in March, BÜKOOP kept the store open, but indoor shopping was considered risky, and customers were not allowed inside. Instead, a list of items available at the time was put on the door, and volunteers then delivered the request of the buyers at the doorstep of the co-op. When the lockdowns started, BÜKOOP volunteers began to discuss how to continue the operations of the co-op and ensure its survival under this period of unprecedented difficulty. Soon, like many other countries in the world, Turkey started to implement stay-at-home measures. University campuses were closed, and a switch to online education took place. BÜKOOP volunteers asked special permission from the university to enter into the campus and open the co-op from time to time, and they were given this permission since BÜKOOP is a food co-operative. A 'pre-payment system' is devised, according to which volunteers and buyers made advance payments and continued to shop for themselves and for others (e.g. their friends, families, and neighbours) from the co-op to ensure its survival. One of us (Özlem), for instance, remembers her trips to the campus during this period of stay-at-home measures as follows: "The very first time, I felt quite emotional. The campus was totally deserted, a bit scary even. I entered into the co-op, and I saw all the food there, all 'clean' and 'just' as we so much cared for, and the only non-food item that we sell in the co-op: soap (from olive oil). I remember I felt in my bones that what we are doing in the co-op is something so right and precious. Apart from these quite exceptional feelings, being able to buy food supplies from the co-operative for my neighbours who could not go out because of the age curfew also felt very good." Such combined efforts of the volunteers in turn meant that they managed to keep the co-op alive during the pandemic, though predictably sales volume dropped substantially.

On the side of the producers, we see that "COVID-19 measures affected the agricultural sector in Turkey in many ways, as the pandemic coincided with both the planting and harvest seasons for different crops. In the fields, workers risked exposure to the virus and had to practice social distancing and wear masks" (Atalan-Helicke and Abiral, 2021, 95). Furthermore, the agriculture sector was not included in the Economic Stability Shield programme designed by the government to provide financial help during the crisis (Atalan-Helicke and Abiral, 2021, 95). Additionally, restrictions on intercity travel and age-based curfews (for those aged over 65 years and younger than 20 years) had consequences as well. One producer BÜKOOP used to work with since the beginning, for instance, decided to move to another city and decrease his engagement with agricultural production to a minimum. This producer cannot send his products (dried fruits, which were popular amongst students) to the co-op since.

BÜKOOP could open the store as previously (twice a day, at noon and in the evening) only starting from Fall 2022. While trying to recover from the pandemic, this time the severe economic crisis that the country is in, the extremely high inflation rates in particular (around 80% for 2022), has begun to pose additional challenges. The prices of the products keep changing so rapidly that it makes one dizzy even to try to follow them. The volunteer that prepares a price list to be posted on the web has to update the list almost daily. The prices of some items (e.g., a specific type of goat cheese) have become so expensive that it sparked a discussion at the co-op whether or not BÜKOOP should continue to have this item on the list. Further increasing the prices is the skyrocketing shipment costs, which were already a considerable burden for BÜKOOP while trying to set a fair price for the products, in addition to its more manageable but still annoying aspects such as broken containers and other cargo delivery problems. Here, an important issue we need to underline is how discussions of what a fair price is unfold: For BÜKOOP, a fair price means that it is fair for both producers and consumers. When producers inform the co-op about prices, the discussion is on whether the price reflects the costs of production so that the farmers can earn just prices, and whether co-op members can afford the prices for particular products. For instance, on various occasions, members discussed the prioritization of certain staple products such as grains and flour over niche products when their prices were regarded to be too high. On other occasions, members, particularly product volunteers, contacted producers to ensure product prices are fair for farmers themselves.

Constantly changing prices and the pandemic meant that BÜKOOP began accepting credit cards again (BÜKOOP had accepted credit cards for a while in its early months but had stopped doing so due to high rates charged by the banks for each transaction). The high rate of inflation, however, made it unpractical to accept cash only, let alone the changes in risk perceptions introduced by the pandemic. Another coping strategy *vis-à-vis* the economic crisis has been to introduce special discounts to students. The campaign called 'citrus fruits to students' (*öğrenciye narenciye* in Turkish), for instance, is designed to sell oranges and other citrus fruits to students half-priced, the associated margin being accounted for jointly by the producers and BÜKOOP volunteers and non-student buyers. Yet another practice involves the aforementioned voluntary advance payment system, in which those members who are willing and can afford to pay in advance ensure cash flow to the co-op so that it becomes possible to continue to buy from the producers. What these practices manifest is how the search for multiple mechanisms of economic transactions without compromising its ideals has become a crucial component of BÜKOOP's resilience.

As if the hurdles stemming from the pandemic and the economic crisis are not enough, BÜKOOP encountered other challenges. One concerned the change in the university administration in 2021. The new university administration embarked upon a reconstruction project in the North campus where the co-op is located. This meant that Baraka, the co-op store, was closed down and demolished. Yet, with the perseverance and commitment of its members, the co-op was able to secure a new location in the same campus. The emotions of the volunteers run high during the move from Baraka to the new space. "It was a historic day," one volunteer commented. "We had so many memories in Baraka," she sighed. The volunteers, nevertheless, made the new space 'theirs' again, by even doing the demanding cleaning after construction themselves. BÜKOOP now continues its operations in this new address, although it had to close its doors temporarily again (for a week) since devastating earthquakes that shook eastern Anatolia in February 2023 affected volunteers and consumers in many diverse ways.

It is perhaps atypical that one catastrophe follows another in such a short period of time, but still it can be argued that BÜKOOP's resilience, mostly thanks to the heartfelt efforts of its volunteers, has been remarkable. The following views of a volunteer in this respect is very revealing and noteworthy: "When I think about the co-op, I always dream a warm environment that volunteers, students can chat, have a cup of tea. On the 'Loooong Saturday' weekend that we took that nice picture, for example, the one with a laughter, many people had visited the co-op, and it was so nice and precious to see that we can still laugh despite all challenges and difficulties. Initially, I was demoralized thinking that they squeezed us to this corner, here at this new place, in the middle of ongoing heavy constructions. But I was touched when I saw that people did find the new place of BÜKOOP in the middle of all this debris and continue to come here, despite the prices increased I don't know how many fold . . . BÜKOOP must have a very special place in people's hearts."

Tension between 'dreams' and 'realities'

We have stated earlier that the relevant literature (e.g. Parkins and Craig, 2009) sees establishing a direct link between farmers and consumers as a key step in building alternative food systems. Face-to-face communication and direct links with producers are indeed very important for BÜKOOP, as emphasized in the following remarks of a volunteer: "If someone is curious about a certain product feature, we can instantly call and ask the producer about the specifics. This breaks the alienation between the producer and the consumer; in the consumer's eyes the producer becomes 'a real person' and vice versa." Interestingly, this direct experience also enables a realistic approach towards producers: "We have seen that they are neither perfect, romantic farmers – like some food activists tend to see them – nor are they 'foxy' individuals as it is commonly assumed in this country. They are people like you and me.

Knowing the producer directly gives us an opportunity to establish a real relationship," states a volunteer. Farmers, on their part, have also benefited from this direct link. Thanks to mutual trust established by close contact over the years, one farmer the co-op works with, for instance, has recently found it unnecessary to obtain an official organic certificate, serving to realize a long-term goal of BÜKOOP: PGS based on mutual trust (BÜKOOP Newsletter, February 2012, 2).

In addition to farm visits, direct communication between farmers and co-op members is also facilitated by the very existence of the co-op store, which became a meeting and learning place for both sides. The co-op store has a sales section and a storage section and serves as a social space not only where food is sold twice a day but also where all members, active volunteers, and farmers can drop by; volunteer for tasks, if they have time, join the co-op meetings or just exchange ideas. In addition to daily shifts, the co-op also remains open on the first Saturday of each month, and reminding Hoffmann's (2016, 164) description of feeling 'a part of a family' or 'finding a home' while working in a co-operative, the day starts with a brunch made collectively in the co-op. In these 'Loooong Saturdays,' volunteers can do some less popular tasks such as cleaning and packaging collectively and keeping the co-op open for shoppers for longer hours. It has been underlined in the literature (Oba and Özsoy, 2020, 366) that such events as New Year celebrations, anniversaries, workshops, and picnics might serve to communicate and share the ideals of AFNs. "These events also provide opportunities for networking and extending the boundaries of their political work. They have a dual function; they reinforce solidarity among in-group members and facilitate the inclusion of newcomers, thus securing enlargement. They signify bonding with people who have a similar worldview and are devoted to the pre-figurative ideas, and provide a space where strategies for future steps are discussed and shaped" (Oba and Özsoy, 2020, 366).

The existence of a co-op store is, therefore, especially important in the creation of a public sphere since it functions as a meeting place for volunteers, consumers, and producers to talk and exchange information and ideas. As such, the co-op store has indeed become a 'commons' (Amin and Howell, 2016) where principles of the co-op are reinforced, a public space where food is discussed, and where university hierarchy gets overturned as people start to know each other better (BÜKOOP Newsletter November/December 2014, 7). The importance of 'working together' is of particular concern in this respect in that students, professors, and administrative personnel working together in the co-op on an equal basis and developing friendships in time contribute to the creation of such an environment.

At the same time, alternative food movements and food co-ops are valuable grounds to better understand diverse economies with regard to possible tensions between 'intentions' and 'practice.' Gritzas and Kavoulakos (2016, 927) argue, for instance, that a close examination of different types of AFNs as a case in the "hidden 'neverland' of diverse economies" can provide crucial insights on the "debate about alterity and diverse economies issues together with contradictions between intentions and practices." Particularly, a focus on the "neglected elements of the economic process" food co-ops rely on, as well as creative interventions they can initiate, might provide a fertile ground to elaborate the expansion of possibilities that food co-ops can offer for a heterogeneous economy (Little et al., 2010, 1799).

"BÜKOOP has managed to build a good fit between 'daily operations' and 'ideals' of the co-op," in the words of a member. According to another, "this has become possible thanks to the fact that there have been tense discussions on this issue." It has been realized, for instance, that the sensitivity over goal displace-ment does not mean that daily operations are unimportant. "It is easy to say broad, general things about co-ops; capitalism is bad and all that. But nothing happens automatically," warns one volunteer; "you need good organization, and organizing tiny little details requires a lot of effort," he concludes. Exemplifying Stryjan's (1994) conceptualization of members' organizations, the same volun-teer highlights a very interesting dimension of the issue and states that the way volunteers tackle everyday practices has, in fact, moved the co-op closer to its ideals in that "the founding principles of BÜKOOP have been fleshed out and given substance to, by the way they were put into practice."

Flexibility becomes a key issue while managing the tensions between 'inten-tions' and 'practice.' Treating decisions as provisional (Leach, 2016) and hav-ing some flexibility and adoptability (Chen, 2016) while acknowledging the necessity of good planning have indeed proved effective for the co-op: "We have learnt to be flexible; following our principles not in words but in deed," says a volunteer. "We prefer to work with organized farmers, for example. We have repeatedly seen that on paper something might look perfect, say a producer co-op. But when you visit the place, it may turn out that it is a one-person show, not a real co-op," he explains. It is also possible to see just the opposite, an interesting example for which is a cheese producer located in Kars, with whom BÜKOOP has been working since its foundation in 2009. This producer is on paper, not a co-operative but a company. However, the owner supports the idea of food co-ops so much so that he does not only make a good discount for the sales made to consumer food co-operatives but being an important and leading figure in the region, he also organizes other producers and farmers as well as actively promoting ecological farming. And yet, one volunteer, who agrees that some flexibility might indeed be required in the co-op, warns that there should be a limit in this respect: "For example, a couple of years ago we have stopped using an independent software and started to use a commercial software pro-gramme instead. I agree that the former was creating problems but still, this is a concession from our principles. Examples like this should remain as an excep-tion, I think, or else there will be a real risk of goal displacement."

Considerable time is required to deeply discuss the tension between 'ide-als' and 'practical necessities.' Such discussions are conducted sometimes via online groups of the co-op but typically during regular meetings, where decisions are taken on a consensus basis. If it is not possible to reach a consensus, the matter is then not pursued. This might mean it takes considerable time till volunteers convince each other, until nobody has a reservation or hesitation on a given issue; hence, we see another reflection of the motto of 'slow co-op' here. Accordingly, we can state that practices that aim for solidarity and inclusion guide the governance practices of the co-op, which is a non-hierarchical and horizontal organization. As stated by a volunteer of BÜKOOP, "everyone who contributes with their labour to the co-operative has an equal right in the decision-making process." This approach to decision-making distinguishes new generation co-operatives from the conventional co-operatives in Turkey with an explicit reference to being transparent, inclusive, and participatory (Oba and Özsoy, 2020, 361). Importantly, a last note in this regard is that not only the discussions but also the tension involved in these discussions is good to have, according to a volunteer: "It is good to have this tension since it paves the way for interesting discussions and contributes positively to the co-op in the end. I have learnt a lot from these tensions. I believe it is healthy, and it shouldn't go away," she explains.

BÜKOOP's success or what it means to be 'a successful consumer food co-op'?

BÜKOOP has had reservations for growth from the beginning and consciously limits itself in this respect. In the words of one BÜKOOP member, "if your targets are useful and small, such as relying on few producers that you can trust, then ideals and reality fit together. If the co-op grows, perhaps we will be able to buy certain products cheaper. However, it may also lead to compromising our criteria in the choice of producers that we buy from." BÜKOOP's choice instead is to create an alternative model that strengthens awareness and solidarity with regard to politics of food and, by so doing, inspire others and share its experience so that similar alternative organizations (which might be potential network partners) can be established elsewhere rather than growing into a giant organization itself.

At the same time, this deliberate choice to stay small is viewed as crucial to maintain the meaning of collective labour devoted to the co-op and to prevent the concentration of power, as exemplified in the following remarks of a volunteer: "When there is money and rent with growth, and if voluntary labour is abandoned, there will be hierarchy, and things will start to deteriorate." A larger size might indeed necessitate hiring professional workers, which, as stated by a member, is likely to "kill volunteerism and perhaps risk maintaining the co-op spirit since certain individuals might begin to act like 'they are the owners,' and power games might begin." Currently, he continues, "we all know that BÜKOOP belongs to us all. This reinforces trust, ensures that thefts and things like that are of negligible amount." "This kind of volunteer energy is only possible if you are small," argues another member, confirming

Rothschild-Whitt's (1979) idea that direct democratic forms relying on volunteerism and face-to-face relations are hard to maintain if the organization grows beyond a certain size and Leach's (2016) emphasis on the benefits of avoiding paid staff.

"But it does make a difference for the producer how much you buy from them; so, you need to find a balance," a volunteer adds, reminding the associated costs. The choice to remain small has indeed some costs. It means, for instance, that the co-op could only be open for certain hours during the day, when there are volunteers to open it. It might also mean that the co-op faces difficulties in obtaining certain product categories at accessible prices. Besides, in many instances, the co-op's purchases do not suffice to make a difference for the farmers. The experience of BÜKOOP then reveals not only that 'small is beautiful' but also that 'it is not sufficient' since, in order to reach a scale that makes a difference for producers, the need for a network organization of co-ops is repeatedly underlined. This is not an easy task, however. Although BÜKOOP has inspired several other university and neighbourhood co-ops, it seems that reaching a scale that will make a difference for farmers beyond a symbolic value will take some time.

BÜKOOP's distinctive approach to growth has links to the debates revolving around de-growth as well, given that being a member of a consumer co-operative is seen amongst the practices providing evidence of a core de-growth economic culture in formation (Kallis et al., 2012). The question of "to what extent such practices can constitute the core of a de-growth economy," however, requires paying attention to the challenge that co-ops face in terms of making a meaningful change in both consumers' and producers' livelihoods. As pointed out by Schneider et al. (2010, 515), this will, in turn, determine "whether such initiatives will inevitably remain on the fringe of the economy or whether they provide real alternatives that can be scaled up and provide the building blocks of a future de-growth society." BÜKOOP's above-discussed path with respect to its approach to growth, emphasizing being sceptical towards growing into a giant organization itself but encouraging co-operation of co-operatives, is inspiring in this regard as well.

It seems that the co-op tries to be sufficiently big to survive economically but stay sufficiently small to be run by volunteers and protect the 'co-op spirit.' Co-op spirit is perceived as continually constructed through ongoing deliberation; "from the very beginning, we have proceeded forward through talking and learning. Talking has fed the whole process," in the words of a volunteer. This also relates to Chen's (2016, 86) point that "discussions about principles and practices also are crucial to enhancing participatory practices' support of authentic voice and engagement." The online co-op e-mail group works as a platform facilitating the process of decision-making, whereas the WhatsApp group of the co-op (*Beyaz Masa*) is very effective in organizing daily operations.

In terms of embodiment of the co-op spirit, BÜKOOP members underline the importance of solidarity, trust, doing collective and voluntary work, being inclusive, learning and deciding together, and having a positive attitude. 'Working together' in particular has been much emphasized and is believed to be extremely effective in building and maintaining a co-op spirit. "Organizing via working together is crucial for building a co-op spirit; it is the key," says a member. Writing on 'the language of BÜKOOP' (on the web page of the co-op, www.bukoop.org), one volunteer underlines that 'our style of working' becomes the 'language' itself, spoken by different volunteers with their own accents, which reflects the diversity of members. This emphasis on embracing diversity and being inclusive is of special importance given the intensity of the debate revolving around accessibility and inclusiveness (Kohn, 2002). Besides, even unpopular work, such as cleaning the co-op, might acquire meaning when conducted collectively (Chen, 2016, 88), and we know that people feel less alienated when engaged in collectivist work (Rothschild-Whitt and Whitt, 1986, 313). Relatedly, not following a top-down approach towards newcomers is as important as avoiding the image of 'a closed group of friends,' states another member: "You shouldn't start with the importance of food sovereignty to a first-comer, s/he will run away. Working together, through collective work, we start to talk naturally about these issues." Another volunteer agrees: "It doesn't work so well when you try to convey a message by just saying it; you need to do it. Otherwise, it gives the feeling that 'I am an expert and now telling you how to do it,' often with no result." Actually, we should perhaps underline, at this juncture, a lesson that BÜKOOP has taught us: In a university context where everybody is an expert on something, be it designing web pages or alternative food movements or organization theory, extreme care is needed to be able to build and maintain an inclusive style.

Keeping the co-op spirit alive is as crucial as building it. "We continue to work in the co-op with the same level of enthusiasm, the same level of excitement like in the first day," describes a volunteer who is amongst the founders of the co-op. Active volunteers play a key role in keeping the co-op spirit alive by continuously reminding things to do, encouraging other volunteers, or sometimes just by chatting and joking in online message groups. "The buddy system contributes to maintaining the co-op spirit as well," underlines a member. The buddy system involves having two volunteers (usually, one 'old' and one 'new') working together for a particular task. In this way, the new volunteer both learns the specifics of the task and also internalizes what kind of a place the co-op is. The co-op spirit is, in other words, successfully transferred to newcomers who are trained by volunteers when they first join the co-op, enabling the re-production of co-op values in line with Stryjan (1994). The importance attributed to the co-op spirit also guides the co-op in terms of setting its strategic priorities. For example, as mentioned earlier, BÜKOOP has rejected demands from the alumni for online shopping and shipment since the desired relation between a member and the co-op is not a 'remote' one; members are, in this way, encouraged to visit the co-op and 'breathe' the co-op spirit as well as contributing to it. "We prioritize face-to-face contact, which feeds the co-op spirit," explains a volunteer.

Building and maintaining a co-op spirit is a real achievement of BÜKOOP. It serves towards attracting new volunteers as well. A new volunteer gives the presence of the co-op spirit as the main reason why she has joined the co-op. "I feel good when in the co-op. The positive atmosphere here attracts the right kind of people," she underlines. Positive emotions, therefore, do indeed seem to further solidarity (Hoffmann, 2016, 154). In a similar vein, another volunteer states that she feels sad when she is busy and cannot volunteer for the co-op: "When I am in the co-op, volunteering, I do not want to leave, I feel happy. I know other volunteers feel the same." For many volunteers, working once or twice a month in the co-op fulfils an emotional need. As Zwerdling (1979, 98) reminds, "a sense of communion, drinking tea, and talking while slicing up wheels of cheese all seek to satisfy human needs forgotten in the plastic-coated world of a corporate supermarket." BÜKOOP has been very rewarding for volunteers in this regard. This also relates to Furman and Papavasiliou's (2018, 184) discussion of affect in local food movement that goes beyond emotions of individuals and focus on affect as it "points to the shared sentiments that envelope agents and guide their conduct and action within the movement." In their words, "economic realities emerge from reflexive and intersubjective structures of feeling that give meaning to activity and render people into particular kinds of economic subjects, who in turn materialize economic ideologies into the realm of experience" (Furman and Papavasiliou, 2018, 181).

We confirm from our direct experience that emotional satisfaction and joy associated with volunteering do strengthen the co-op spirit, and "a taste of participation leads to the desire for more" (Rothschild-Whitt and Whitt, 1986, 307). This is of key importance since, while discussing alienation, Marx attributes a special meaning to working "with a willing hand, a ready mind, and a joyous heart" (Rothschild-Whitt and Whitt, 1986, 305). Breaking alienation, Rothschild (2016, 26) argues, can be achieved if the individual is allowed "to be able to develop authentic feelings of pride in the work product and solidarity in the work process with others." An illustrative example from the producers' side comes from the Vakıflı co-op (see the next chapter for a detailed analysis of this co-op). It is a women's co-operative that produces handmade jams and syrups. Every product had an assigned number indicating the woman who produced it. This practice facilitated planning and made it convenient for both co-ops to deal with any problems/demands about the product. For BÜKOOP members, however, it was also very important to know who produced a given product, as this allowed recognition of the human labour in production. When such a system is used, the product itself is stripped away from being a mere object of consumption and regains its genuine value, including that of the human labour involved in its production. Even though Vakıflı co-op recently abandoned this practice since they switched to collective production in their common kitchen, developing a mechanism that will enable having more information about the producers on the etiquettes of the products is an ongoing discussion amongst BÜKOOP members.

Establishing an organizational system with adequate size that works, that enables taking decisions on a consensus basis and feeds participation amongst volunteers, that ensures solidarity-based relations with farmers, and that provides enough revenue to run the place are all amongst the other achievements of BÜKOOP, which has become a model to emulate. When asked about if they think BÜKOOP is successful, all volunteers we interviewed agreed that it is, emphasizing its sustainability above all in that surviving for 14 years without sacrificing its principles is considered a success in and of itself. "I don't know any other examples around, of a similar organization that is based on volunteer work, maintains its principles, and has survived for so many years," explains a volunteer. "BÜKOOP is a working model of an alternative organization. It transforms ordinary people's lives, it politicizes them," underlines another member. "The fact that we do well financially is a blessing, too; it gives us confidence as well as a firm base to realize our goals," adds a volunteer. Yet another volunteer describes how his perception in this regard evolved over time: "In the beginning I was very optimistic. Over time, I have realized how difficult it is to do collective work. But we did it; we managed to establish a trust-based organization." A related remark comes from another volunteer who states that she was rather sceptical about collective work before joining the co-op: "It gives me hope to see in the co-op that collective work is possible. You know, such groups often dissolve because of silly reasons. The fact that this has not happened here is a success of BÜKOOP."

In a study that analyses BÜKOOP, Kaya (2019, 1440) observes that the co-op is careful in gender-related aspects as well. No task is considered to be gender-specific, and all work is shared regardless of the volunteers' affiliation (i.e. student, professor, or administrative staff) or gender. This is especially of vital importance while conducting unpopular tasks such as cleaning. The co-op, however, applies positive discrimination for women co-operatives. One example is a women's co-op that BÜKOOP prefers to work with, despite knowing very well that they procure the ingredients from local bazaars (not from carefully selected farmers as BÜKOOP expects) to produce their products like tomato paste. This point, apart from illustrating the importance attributed to women's co-op, is also telling in terms of the previously mentioned flexibility of BÜKOOP (perhaps another motto emerges here: 'Flexible co-op'), always emphasizing its core values but reshuffling its priorities around these core values when necessary.

Continuous support of the Farmers' Union to BÜKOOP since its foundation, be it publicly in national press or on its website, contributes positively towards BÜKOOP's success according to Kaya (2019, 1443), who also underlines the contribution of the good reputation of the Boğaziçi University and its possible benefits in this respect. In fact, the co-operative store's being in campus not only provides advantages ranging from safety to being visible and easily accessible to Boğaziçi students and staff, but it also means that its reach to a wider range of consumers remains restricted. Nevertheless, the 'success' of BÜKOOP is praised not only by the consumers, producers, and volunteers of BÜKOOP themselves but also in the academic studies conducted on BÜKOOP. Soysal Al (2020, 144), for instance, writes the following in this regard:

> The co-operative's contribution to supporting small-scale ecological farming and its efforts toward affordably healthy food for consumers is significant, especially because it is a pioneering example for the similar co-operatives that emerged in the following years, in particular the Kadıköy Co-op that opened the first neighbourhood-scale ecological consumer food co-operative in Istanbul. . . . This is an exemplary organization model on a campus that motivates young people to become agents with their own voice in an agro-food context that severely threatens their future and health and to communize the politics of foods as citizens through horizontal, participative, and democratic relations.

In a similar vein, Kaya (2019, 1441) states that BÜKOOP played a pioneering role in encouraging the foundation of new consumer co-ops and generated solutions to the problems of small producers. Besides, with its sensitivity on the issue, BÜKOOP has contributed problematizing 'organic' consumption and certification by defending the right to healthy and just food for all. The last point of success for BÜKOOP, according to Kaya (2019, 1441), is establishing long-term, trust-based relations with producers. With these characteristics, BÜKOOP is argued to qualify as a 'socially innovative' organization, especially with regard to how the co-operative chooses producers and organizes producer–consumer relations, the way it functions, the way volunteers communicate, and the way all these reflected to the consumers. By doing so, Kaya (2019, 1446) concludes, BÜKOOP addresses a social need and contributes to the mobilization potential of the society for a better future.

Nevertheless, BÜKOOP has its own unique problems, ambivalences, and challenges. The choice to remain small, for instance, has some costs, as already discussed earlier. As predicted in the literature (Hoffmann, 2016; Rothschild-Whitt and Whitt, 1986), instances of individuals getting burned out are of concern as well. Several volunteers of BÜKOOP have experienced burnout over the course of 14 years. One founding member who suffered the first burnout describes his experience as follows: "We all dream wonderful things but when it comes to putting an effort, very few people are actually around. Most work then is left to the shoulders of a few people, who have to carry the burden. This in turn causes burnout." "During the first two years, most of the work used to be handled by 3–4 people, which was unsustainable. Fortunately, new volunteers came, and we recovered. There is still a core group but now it is larger, and many other volunteers put their labour, too," adds another member.

Also relevant in this respect are emotional debts, which may "contribute to social bonding but also result in interactional barriers with others" (Hale and Carolan, 2018, 125). We observe such emotional debts amongst BÜKOOP volunteers when, for instance, one volunteer asks for a replacement when s/he cannot go to a shift or cannot be ready to meet the cargo shipment of a product s/he is responsible for. Such emotional debts have not created any visible problems for BÜKOOP volunteers so far, but it is not hard to predict that if one individual willingly or unwillingly carries too much emotional debt, it might eventually lead to burnout.

Importantly, individuals' attitudes also seem to matter in this respect: "You do things, people see you do them, and they begin to leave everything to you. Volunteering then becomes kind of mandatory for you. And you fed up after a point," says the volunteer who has experienced the first burnout. "I wonder what would happen if a volunteer on the verge of a burnout, instead of taking initiative immediately, just declared s/he quit a specific task to see if another volunteer would assume responsibility," muses a member. The experience of BÜKOOP reveals mixed evidence in this regard. It worked, for instance, when the volunteer who has experienced the first burnout complained about burnout. His complaint triggered a collective search for remedies, resulting in other volunteers sharing some of his tasks. But this method did not work in the case of the co-op bulletin, which could not be published for some time since the volunteer who was editing the bulletin went for a sabbatical, and nobody assumed responsibility for the task. Relatedly, there are various ways in which members, who have less time to give, can contribute to the co-op, if not anything, by just shopping from the co-op from time to time. A specific example in this regard is the aforementioned practice of 'Loooong Saturdays.' Accordingly, the co-op remains open between 11:30 a.m. and 02:30 p.m. on the first Saturday of each month so that collective work could be done by the volunteers, and those who could not make it during weekdays (e.g. alumni) could have an opportunity to contribute.

According to a volunteer, building rules and procedures, that is, building a 'system' as the volunteers describe it, has helped the co-op enormously: "All this taught us the importance of organization and establishing systems, which could work independent of certain individuals." BÜKOOP, as a result, developed detailed recording systems. Volunteers, for example, use the so-called yellow notebook to record every bit of relevant information during the shifts, and a volunteer is supposed to record everything (e.g. delivery details, prices, and transportation costs) about the product, for which s/he is responsible, in the relevant computer files.

The number of active volunteers may fluctuate at any given period for BÜKOOP. This may have some relation with it being a university-based co-op, amongst other things. Regarding student volunteers, for instance, volunteering time might be affected given outgoing and graduating students and the intense course schedule current students might have during certain times of the term. For volunteers who are administrative staff members, on the other hand, official office hours pose a limit, whereas academic volunteers might take a sabbatical leave or simply retire. All this does not only underline again the key importance of building effective systems that work independent of specific individuals as mentioned earlier but also introduces limits in the operations of the co-op, an example being limited working hours, which have of course consequences: They possibly restrict the number of consumers and, in turn, the volume of products ordered from producers (Soysal Al, 2020, 143).

A final note in this regard concerns the importance attributed to core values which are, in the words of a volunteer "care about social, economic, ecologic inequalities in agriculture . . . and aim to provide fairly priced, clean of pesticides, local products directly from small producers to consumers that eliminate the intermediaries" (Oba and Özsoy, 2020, 360). These core values are shared by and inspired other consumer co-ops as well, which are linked in the literature to these co-ops' nature as grassroots movements shaped around collective identities. In the words of a volunteer: "We share our experiences with many groups but not all of them are able to implement them. There must be a political formation to support and be involved in the movement. There must be ideals about how to get organized and a culture to nourish the movement" (Oba and Özsoy, 2020, 360), a point supporting the line of the relevant literature emphasizing the link of AFN organizations to the food movement (Türkkan, 2021).

Regarding the issue of 'success' then, it can safely be concluded that achievements of BÜKOOP far exceed the aforementioned concerns in its functioning. It has made significant progress towards its aims and managed to survive for 14 years without sacrificing these aims, despite all challenges, and above all has managed to develop and maintain a 'co-op spirit' shared by the volunteers, consumers, and producers alike.

References

Amin, A., & Howell, P. (2016). Thinking the commons. In A. Amin & P. Howell (eds.) *Releasing the Commons: Rethinking the Futures of the Commons* (pp. 1–17). Routledge.

Atalan-Helicke, N., & Abiral, B. (2021). Alternative food distribution networks, resilience, and urban food security in Turkey during the COVID-19 pandemic. *Journal of Agriculture, Food Systems, and Community Development*, 10(2), 89–104. https://doi.org/10.5304/jafscd.2021.102.021

Chen, K. K. (2016). Plan your burn, burn your plan: How decentralization, storytelling, and communification can support participatory practices. *The Sociological Quarterly*, 57, 71–97. https://doi.org/10.1111/tsq.12115

Furman, C. A., & Papavasiliou, F. (2018). Scale and affect in the local food movement. *Food, Culture & Society*, 21(2), 180–195. https://doi.org/10.1080/15528014.2018.1427926

Gritzas, G., & Kavoulakos, K. I. (2016). Diverse economies and alternative spaces: An overview of approaches and practices. *European Urban and Regional Studies*, 23(4), 917–934. https://doi.org/10.1177/0969776415573778

Hale, J., & Carolan, M. (2018). Co-operative or uncooperative cooperatives? Digging into the process of co-operation in food and agriculture co-operatives. *Journal of Agriculture, Food Systems, and Community Development*, 8(1), 113–132. https://doi.org/10.5304/jafscd.2018.081.011

Hoffmann, E. A. (2016). Emotions and emotional labour at worker-owned businesses: Deep acting, surface acting, and genuine emotions. *The Sociological Quarterly*, 57, 152–173. https://doi.org/10.1111/tsq.12113

Kallis, G., Kerschner, C., & Martinez-Alier, J. (2012). The economics of de-growth. *Ecological Economics*, 84, 172–180. https://doi.org/10.1016/j.ecolecon.2012.08.017

Kaya, Ç. (2019). Sosyal iş modelleri ve sosyal girişimcilik: Boğaziçi Üniversitesi Tüketim Kooperatifi örneği. *İşletme Araştırmaları Dergisi*, 11(3), 1433–1449.

Kohn, M. (2002). Panacea or privilege? New approaches to democracy and association. *Political Theory*, 30(2), 289–298. https://doi.org/10.1177/0090591702030002

Leach, D. K. (2016). When freedom is not an endless meeting: A new look at efficiency in consensus-based decision making. *The Sociological Quarterly*, 57, 36–70. https://doi.org/10.1111/tsq.12137

Little, R., Maye, D., & Ilbery, B. (2010). Collective purchase: Moving local and organic foods beyond the niche market. *Environment and Planning A*, 42, 1797–1813. https://doi.org/10.1068/a4262

Mooney, P. H. (2004). Democratizing rural economy: Institutional friction, sustainable struggle and the cooperative movement. *Rural Sociology*, 69(1), 76–98. https://doi.org/10.1526/003601104322919919

Oba, B., & Özsoy, Z. (2020). Unifying nature of food: Consumer-initiated cooperatives in Istanbul. *Society and Business Review*, 15(4), 349–372. https://doi.org/10.1108/SBR-07-2019-0100

Parkins, W., & Craig, G. (2009). Culture and the politics of alternative food networks. *Food, Culture & Society*, 12(1), 77–103. https://doi.org/10.2752/155280109X368679

Rosol, M. (2020). On the significance of alternative economic practices: Reconceptualizing alterity in alternative food networks. *Economic Geography*, 96(1), 52–76. https://doi.org/10.1080/00130095.2019.1701430

Rothschild, J. (2016). The logic of a co-operative economy and democracy 2.0: Recovering the possibilities for autonomy, creativity, solidarity, and common purpose. *The Sociological Quarterly*, 57, 7–35. https://doi.org/10.1111/tsq.12138

Rothschild-Whitt, J. (1979). Conditions for democracy: Making organizations work. In J. Case & R. J. R. Taylor (eds.) *Co-ops, Communes & Collectives: Experiments in Social Change* (pp. 215–244). Pantheon Books.

Rothschild-Whitt, J., & Whitt, J. A. (1986). Worker-owners as an emergent class: Effects of cooperative work on job satisfaction, alienation, and stress. *Economic and Industrial Democracy*, 7, 297–317. https://doi.org/10.1177/0143831X8673004

Schneider, F., Kallis, G., & Martinez-Alier, J. (2010). Crisis or opportunity? Economic de-growth for social equity and ecological sustainability. Introduction to this special issue. *Journal of Cleaner Production*, 18, 511–518. https://doi.org/10.1016/j.jclepro.2010.01.014

Soysal Al, I. (2020). The promising momentum and collective practices of the recently expanding network of consumer-led ecological food initiatives in Turkey.

İstanbul Üniversitesi Sosyoloji Dergisi, 40(1), 129–162. https://doi.org/10.26650/SJ.2020.40.1.0046

Soysal AI, I., & Küçük, B. (2019). In-between anxiety and hope: Trusting an alternative among 'alternatives' in the (post) organic food market in Turkey. *International Journal of Sociology of Agriculture & Food*, 25(2), 173–190. https://doi.org/10.48416/ijsaf.v25i2.42

Stryjan, Y. (1994). Understanding co-operatives: The reproduction perspective. *Annals of Public and Co-operative Economics*, 65(1), 59–80.

Türkkan, C. (2020). Feeding the global city: Urban transformation and urban food supply chain in 21st-century Istanbul. *Journal of Urbanism: International Research on Placemaking and Urban Sustainability*, 13(1), 13–37. https://doi.org/10.1080/17549175.2018.1515785

Türkkan, C. (2021). What is the 'alternative'? Insights from Istanbul's food networks. *Food, Culture & Society*, 1–21. https://doi.org/10.1080/15528014.2021.1960004

Zwerdling, D. (1979). The uncertain revival of food co-operatives. In J. Case & R. J. R. Taylor (eds.) *Co-ops, Communes & Collectives: Experiments in Social Change* (pp. 89–111). Pantheon Books.

3 The experience of a producer food co-op

Vakıflı co-op

The history of the Vakıflı co-op

Vakıflı is a village of the Armenian community located in the Hatay Province on the Mediterranean coast of Turkey, near the Syrian border. Hatay is one of Turkey's most religiously, ethnically, and linguistically diverse provinces. Vakıflı (also known as Vakıfköy) is a district of Samandağ in Hatay, a beach town at the mouth of the Asi River, which was the epicentre of the third strong earthquake that struck that part of the country in February 2023. There were no casualties in Vakıflı, but the quakes left the village's stone houses heavily damaged, and the 130 villagers have been forced to live in tents, not knowing when exactly life in the village could return to some state of normality again. Although its population has already been dwindling due to migration to big cities, mainly driven by economic hardships and education-related reasons, leading some to argue that Vakıflı "could disappear within a generation" (McTighe, 2018), a trend feared to be worsened by the earthquakes, the villagers continue to strive to keep their village, culture, and traditions alive.

The village economy relies on agriculture and, more recently, also on tourism since Vakıflı is attracting tourists with its beautiful views of the surrounding mountains and the Mediterranean Sea, rich history, and culture, as well as its unique agricultural produce. The economic fortunes of Vakıflı were rather limited until the late 1990s, but when the historic church in the village was restored in 1997, both national and international tourism started to gain momentum (McTighe, 2018). Villagers recall that the opening ceremony of the Church was very influential in this respect. Guests arrived from all over the world and Turkey, and national and international media reported the ceremony in detail, which played a key role in attracting the world's attention to the village. A foundation in Istanbul, established by those who are of Vakıflı origin, further contributed to promotion of the village. As a result, Vakıflı, which was a rather unknown and tranquil village until then, has become quite well-known and even 'trendy' in the words of an interviewee, and national and international tour operators began to include Vakıflı in their holiday packages, reinforcing its image and popularity. Another interviewee notes that as the village became more and more known,

DOI: 10.4324/9781003289166-3

daily visitors were asking if there was a hostel they could stay, as they found Vakıflı very beautiful and wanted to stay more, which led to the restoration of three old stone houses to be used as hostels. Hatay Airport was opened in 2007, which significantly improved transportation to Vakıflı. As a final note in this respect, we should underline that Vakıflı has a good potential for eco-tourism as well. In a recent study (Salıcı, 2018, 2713), it has been found that Vakıflı is the route with the highest potential for eco-tourism within the region thanks to its rich natural, cultural, religious, and historical heritage. The fact that the broader area that Vakıflı resides in has been declared as the 'Hatay Samandağ Tourism Zone' in the Tourism Strategy Action Plan of Turkey in the early 1990s since it includes protected areas such as breeding sites for sea turtles and venues of interest for religion-related tourism activities also contributed to the tourism potential of Vakıflı (Salıcı, 2018).

However, despite benefiting from the notable increase in touristic activities in recent decades, the village continues to depend largely on agriculture. About 70 per cent of land in Vakıflı is used for agriculture, mostly for growing fruits and vegetables. All citrus fruits like oranges and lemons are grown in the village, tangerines being the most common. An increase in olive and olive oil production is also observed in the village in recent years. Vakıflı is one of the first places in the region that received organic certification. The transition process towards organic agriculture took about four years and was completed in 2004. In 2005, about one thousand tonnes of organic products from the village were exported to the EU countries (Germany and France, in particular) in addition to being sold in big supermarkets in Turkey (Kuşçu and Tuncel, 2009, 54–55). Vakıflı continued certified organic farming until the year 2009, when it was abandoned, mainly because holding the certificate became too expensive for the villagers. Their products, however, remained ecological. Villagers underline that when certified organic production started in Vakıflı, they initially had positive results, but this did not continue due to high costs, especially the high cost of organic fertilizers, which increased prices enormously. These high prices in turn meant a decrease in demand. In addition, as one of our interviewees indicates, their organic products were highly demanded from Europe, and the best quality were exported, and the remaining products were sold in the domestic market. However, there was not much demand in the domestic market because consumers were questioning the appearance of organic products as they were not standard and not as 'good looking' in terms of colour and shape in comparison to conventional products: "People could not recognize the value of organic production then. We are talking about the 1990s and early 2000s. Now, many people value organic production but then it wasn't the case unfortunately," explains an interviewee. All these facts caused villagers to give up certified organic production.

In terms of agricultural production, golden years of the village were between 1985 and 2000, according to the villagers. Good revenues and profits, hence the 'golden age,' however, faded away with sales becoming increasingly difficult, coupled with the problem of land fragmentation due to inheritance-related issues (Aksoy, 2018, 241–242). Villagers particularly underline that even if the price of the product that the consumer has to pay increases, they cannot benefit from that increase due to systemic reasons, complaining about a very fundamental fact regarding the dominant agricultural system in Turkey, which benefits intermediaries at the expense of producers and consumers. This introduces a vicious circle, where the downfall in agriculture feeds migration to big cities, which has already been underway not only because of economic hardships but also due to the fact that the youth go to universities and prefer the lifestyle in big cities. All this in turn further decreases small-scale agricultural activities in villages like Vakıflı. The village dwellers have been taking precautions to stop migration to big cities, and the Vakıflı Village Agro-Development Co-operative played a significant role in this regard. The co-operative, established in 2004, organizes sales of the fruit grown in the village without a need for any intermediaries, arranges marketing of these products, and provides a platform for discussing agriculture-related problems of farmers. All farmers in the village are members. While the main rationale for establishing the co-operative is economic, it is at the same time a manifestation of collective action and reinforces solidarity amongst villagers, contributing to sustainability and community development in the village.

A women's branch of the co-operative was founded unofficially a year later, in 2005, specializing in producing handmade jams and syrups. This branch would later evolve into the women's co-op, formally established in 2021. Our interviewees emphasize that this did not happen overnight, underlining the long-term labour and commitment behind the women's co-op. One of the founders we interviewed states that the first seeds of the women's co-op can be traced back to the open market (so-called kermes) they set up in the church's garden in the summer of 2005. She notes that this happened as a woman villager came up with the idea to sell homemade products, including the wide variety of liquors, jams, salted yogurt, and pomegranate syrup, that are distinctive and peculiar to the village in order to provide support for the restoration efforts to turn a stone house into a hostel: "She said we should not stay idle, the village needs money. I asked her, what are we going to sell? She said these products are so valuable, they cannot be found anywhere else. We used to offer these to the visitors of our village for free, this time, why not sell them?" Seeing the success of this 'kermes,' the women decided to continue this sale, rather than a one-time event, and that's how the foundation of an 'unofficial' women's branch within the Vakıflı agriculture co-op was initiated, explains our interviewee. Another interviewee underlines that five women pioneered this initiative, and in time, the number of women involved in the women's branch increased substantially. In these initial years, they were mostly selling their products to the visitors of Vakıflı, whose number had increased considerably following the restoration of the church in 1997, as mentioned earlier. The market, in other words, "used to come to us," in the words of one of our interviewees.

In an interview she gave for *BirartıBir* (Çameli, 2020), a founder associates the rationale for specializing in jams and syrups not only with the renowned success of the region in fruit production but also with their local culture, underlining that in Armenian culture, it is common to serve liquor (narcissus liquor in particular) with chocolate. She states that over time they diversified these traditional types of liquor, and now they make liquor from a large variety of fruits. In many respects, Vakıflı resembles other initiatives of a similar nature active in other parts of the world, one example being a co-operative started by 36 women in 1998 in Hidalgo in rural Mexico. Like Vakıflı, this co-operative specializes in the production of syrups, in their case agave syrup, using local agaves (Sato and Soto Alarcón, 2019). The focus on traditional products and methods in Vakıflı also parallels some other women's co-ops studied in the literature, especially those targeting culinary heritage (e.g. Jalkh et al., 2020). At the same time, one of our interviewees underlines the importance of exchange of culinary knowledge between neighbours, different ethnic groups in the region, culminating in a highly qualified Hatay cuisine, which reflects the richness of several cultures coming together in creating this distinctive gastronomy.

As noted earlier, although the women of Vakıflı have been actively working under the Vakıflı Village Agro-Development Co-operative, as a women's branch since 2005, the official establishment of a women's co-op in Vakıflı is quite new. One of our interviewees, who triggered the foundation of the official women's co-op in 2021, explains why and how this need emerged as follows: "In the last couple of years, I noticed an imbalance in terms of the benefits different women could get from the sales. One woman could produce say 30 jars, whereas another could do 100–200 jars. This in effect meant that only 3–5 women could earn serious incomes from the co-op sales, whereas others, the majority in fact, were left behind. Think of it as a pie, one large slice to someone, the rest to all others, it shouldn't be like that, should it?" It should be noted at this juncture that this approach very much reflects issues regarding inclusivity that Bijman and Wijers (2019, 75) discuss as a crucial component of community-oriented rather than market-oriented producer co-operatives. This interviewee, having seen that her observation in this regard is shared by other women in the village, tells how this observation, combined with what she learnt from many seminars and workshops she attended thanks to the Foundation for the Support of Women's Work (KEDV), made her think that this system should change and establishing an official women's co-operative could provide this opportunity. "I asked one of our friends," she goes, "she was working in Agos (an Armenian newspaper) in İstanbul but had just moved back here since she got married. She is a university graduate. I asked her to investigate how we could do it. She did, and we established our official women's co-operative in December 2021," she concludes.

In a similar vein, another interviewee notes the following:

> Before the official women's co-operative, there was a duality between those who could put more capital and thus could produce more, earn more,

and those who couldn't. During the pandemic, however, when sales to tourists practically stopped, since there were hardly any visitors, this problem became more obvious. We also had more time to think about how we could find a way out of this. Establishing an official co-operative, we decided, could enable us to re-organize everything. And that's how we developed a system that enables each member to be equal partners in profit or loss of the co-op, regardless of her means.

In this new system, women benefit from the co-op in two ways: Firstly, as members they get their share at the end of each month from the co-op's profits, which are equally distributed amongst the members; and secondly, they volunteer for daily work in the co-op and get paid for their labour. "In this way, we make sure that each and every house in the village benefits from our common effort in the co-op, while those who work more get additional benefits," she explains. As a result, the previous system, according to which each woman used to produce at home, then deliver whatever she could produce (given her means, economically, knowledge-wise, and/or time-wise) to the women's branch, and get her share from the sales at the end of the month, has now totally changed. One woman from each house in the village, meaning 33 women (there are 35 households in the village, but in two of them there are no women), became members of the official women's co-operative, again demonstrating the emphasis on inclusivity.

"We elected one of our friends as the head of the co-op," an interviewee explains, "another friend is responsible from relations with media," she goes. "We found the most suitable task for everyone. Everybody has an equal share. No one is one step ahead of others. We achieved that, I believe. We have become successful," she concludes. Currently, all women are engaged in the production process, which takes place in the common kitchen in the village. One of our interviewees, who played a central role in this transformation, describes how they initially managed to activate this new system of common production as follows:

To initiate the new system that we designed, we first of all requested advance payments from our members. The co-op needed this seed money from the members to be able to start production. We bought, you know, jars, sugar, all our inputs with this money. We then paid back this 'debt' to our members as soon as the co-op managed to accumulate some revenue from its sales.

It is noteworthy that there is a striking resemblance here to how BÜKOOP initiated its very first operations, for which members' contributions in terms of membership fees played a key role in financing the first products procured by the co-op. Importantly, the same interviewee stresses that the success of the official women's co-op is built upon their experiences in the women's branch:

> I should underline that we did not come to that point in one-and-a half year. We were already producing in the women's branch; we had proved ourselves. I think that we only changed our official status and re-organized our system. We are legally a women's co-op now. We could put women's co-op labels and stickers on our products. We are now walking in our path even more strongly.

The ages of the women who are members of the co-op range from 25 to 60 years. The majority of them are married. More than half of them are secondary school graduates, and the primary school graduates have the lowest rate (about 15%). This level of education is quite high in relative terms when the level of education of women in rural areas in Turkey (about 70% being primary school graduates at most) is considered. Citrus fruits are produced by 70% of the families in the village, and grapes by more than the half. They engage in small-scale production – the average cultivated area per family being about 9 decares (Oruç et al., 2017, 3–5). Most of the sales are typically made to the visitors of Vakıflı and through the network of consumers they acquired with their contacts, quite a number of them being in Istanbul. BÜKOOP is in that latter group. They also cite online orders and/or telephone ordering as growing methods of sale. In fact, telephone orders have become their primary source of income after the pandemic and then the earthquakes, given that tourism to the region has virtually stopped for now. The share of online orders is growing but still very low, mainly because packaging is much more difficult given that online orders are typically very small-scale. "They order one or two jars of jam. You then need to find a suitable package for that, and you do the packaging and then organize the shipment. I am not sure it is worth it. Online sales are symbolic for the time being," explains one of our interviewees.

In our interviews, 'economic freedom for women,' 'contributing to the village,' and 'stopping the migration from the village' are stated as the most important functions of the co-op by the members. They make sure that 80% of the sales goes to the women, and the remaining 20% is spared for the co-op itself to be used for the village. The women of the co-operative name agriculture and co-operative sales as their main sources of income. Above all, thanks to the co-operative, the women feel that they have a voice and a key role in the development of the village, increasing their confidence and self-esteem, since, according to the members, the co-op makes them feel that it is possible to overcome all obstacles and challenges when they join forces, hence their motto 'one for all, all for one.'

Regarding mechanisms of decision-making, it is typical that the board of directors assumes responsibility for daily affairs, but more important decisions are usually left to general meetings. "How much to produce from a particular product, for instance, is a very important decision," explains an interviewee, "I can give the example of last year's decision regarding pomegranate syrup production. How much pomegranate syrup we should produce was not decided by five of us (she means the board of directors). We organized a meeting. Because it is an important decision that needs consultation of all our members," she goes. She then gives another example of a major decision, namely, a decision to buy a new machine. "This again requires a crowded meeting," she explains. This emphasis on making sure to have everybody's voice included in the decision-making process is also reflecting an effort to access the best knowledge available in the co-op. This is important, according to one interviewee, since "sometimes a very innovative idea comes to one of us while just sitting together and talking in these meetings."

When there are differing views, they then vote, and the majority decides. "Even if every member is invited, it is not always the case that all members attend every meeting. In that case, we take the majority of those who participated to that particular meeting," further explains one of our interviewees. She stresses that they continue to follow this method consciously, although they are well aware that it might not necessarily provide the best result always. "We as the board would have liked to produce more pomegranate syrup last year, for example. But the majority decided otherwise, and we produced that agreed amount. But now it is sold out. As I said previously, we are partners both in profit and loss," she concludes.

The role of the co-op in women's empowerment

Echoing the line of the literature investigating the habitual practices and activities of communities in accordance with the seasonal rhythm of farming, which might provide "insights into the factors that tend to be emblematic of successful, enduring, and therapeutic communities" (Liu et al., 2017, 366), there is indeed a seasonal rhythm in tune with nature in Vakıflı. Predictably, daily life revolves around agriculture in the village. Accordingly, the work in the women's co-op is following in parallel to this rhythm. In the words of one of our interviewees:

Every day is not the same in the co-op. There are very busy times and less busy times. We don't prefer to have more than 4–5 women at the common kitchen of the co-op in a given day. It becomes physically disturbing; they cannot even move easily. When working together, women typically gather around the table, do the work, do pickled oregano or whatever, and chat. It's a very social environment. There are of course some extra-crowded, extra-busy days. But there are some other days, during which there is nothing to do. It all depends on the season. It depends on the season of the fruits in question. Whatever fruit is abundant in whatever season, our work intensifies accordingly.

Notably, all work in women's co-op is conducted by the women. This is of particular importance since we know that in the literature there are examples in which women handle the work related to the food itself, such as fruit quality, sorting, and sizing (Meliá-Marti et al., 2020, 4), while men are usually "involved in taking care of the technical infrastructure (website, internet communication system) and standardization of activities (statute, determining rules of operation)," which might indicate, amongst other things, a reproduction of gender inequalities (Kopczyńska, 2017, 15). In the case of the women's co-op in Vakıflı, even technical issues such as online sales are conducted by women. Being able to conduct administrative work in the co-op has enabled some women to explore new roles such as participating in conferences to represent Vakıflı, or organizing and managing meetings, all of which they embrace, paralleling the findings in the literature (Daya and Authar, 2012, 889). Relatedly, when the difficulty of squeezing administrative duties alongside domestic roles is considered, "dividing oneself into two," that is, one part belonging to the co-op and the other to the house (Daya and Authar, 2012, 890), does not seem to be too much of a problem for the women of Vakıflı since they state that, typically, a woman produces syrups and jams to be sold in the co-op by working about four hours a day, leaving a reasonable amount of time for the other parts of their lives. The double shift of household and co-op work is also eased by the fact that it is the men who perform agricultural tasks in the field year around. And yet, the women of Vakıflı call for a recognition of their double efforts, as evident in the following statements of one of our interviewees: "We run all day, between our homes and the co-op. Yet all this hard work at home is invisible. It is as if you don't really work at home since you are not going to a factory or an office. It is in fact very tiring to run all day, both here in the co-op and at home, trying to do everything, taking care of children. But we have to do it. We carry all the burden."

We also learnt about an interesting gender-related dynamic in the village when we asked about the details of why they stopped certified organic production. "Organic production is rather relevant for the agricultural side. We don't do agriculture, we produce jams, syrups, *etc.*, from agricultural products. The other co-operative in the village engages in agricultural production, we call them 'men's co-op.' We typically procure our fruits from the men's co-op," one of our interviewees explained laughing. We dug into that interesting issue and learnt that only women members of the agricultural co-op are those who inherited co-op shares from their husbands, fathers, or brothers, when they ceased to become members. "We are always in contact with the agricultural co-op. We have good relations; they are our husbands, in fact," underlines an interviewee, adding that the women's co-op typically procures olives to make olive oil and fruits like bitter oranges to make jams and syrups from the men's co-op.

Women's newfound economic freedom, thanks to the co-operative, means that they can now contribute to their family income, which strengthens their economic empowerment. In the words of one of our interviewees: "Economic benefits of the co-op are significant. Women began to support their households, their livelihoods. It is reassuring that you know every month you'll get something from the co-op, sometimes a little sometimes more. Maybe 100 liras, maybe 500, or 5,000. Whatever we earn, we share. You feel great because you earn your own money." These accounts confirm the line of the literature stressing that "women's co-operatives also touch women's heart while supporting them economically" (Duguid et al., 2015, 87). Women's stories also reveal that satisfaction derived from being able to use the money they earn for their own consumption or for the consumption of their families means a lot to them, illustrating another dimension of economic empowerment. Personal narratives of 12 women members of the Heiveld, a rooibos producer co-operative in the Northern Cape Province of South Africa, for instance, show that "the first response of several of the women to a general question about their experience of changes since joining the Heiveld is to refer to their pleasure in having their own money and being able to buy things for themselves" (Daya and Authar, 2012, 891). Moreover, ownership of money brings not just the freedom to purchase but also the power to take a more active role in domestic decision-making. In brief, economic empowerment also enables these women to be "autonomous individuals; more equal partners in marriage; respectable members of the community" (Daya and Authar, 2012, 891).

The members of the women's co-op in Vakıflı do benefit from their activities in the co-op not only economically but also socially and psychologically. In fact, according to a survey conducted in the village (Oruç et al., 2017, 8–9), more than 80% consider such benefits to be very important. In our interviews, one striking manifestation of the psychological contributions of working together at the co-op after the devastating earthquakes in February 2023 was articulated by an interviewee as follows: "Economic benefits are of course very important, but it also feels very good to be together, to work together. I can give the example of the aftermath of the earthquakes. When we couldn't recover psychologically, the co-op healed us in a way. We established a common kitchen. In the early days, just after the quakes, we were living together in the tea house. We as the women's co-op made everybody work, participate. Everybody helped us in packaging, for example. You know, working heals you. The co-op therefore provided means for people to recover." All these observations are in line with the growing literature on women's co-operatives in Turkey, highlighting both economic and non-economic benefits – a recent study focusing on women's co-operatives in Turkey (Çınar et al., 2021, 779) and a World Bank report (Duguid et al., 2015, 16) emphasizing the versatility of women's co-operatives in Turkey being two notable examples in this respect.

The co-op also provides opportunities for social contacts for their members, sometimes extending beyond the village. It is a social space, enabling women to escape from the otherwise isolating conditions of staying at home and doing housework all the time (Moon, 2022, 8). Amongst the most important achievements of the women's co-ops, an increase in visibility and status of women has been frequently mentioned, with a particular emphasis on how after joining the co-operative their lives have become more 'colourful' with the co-operative's activities and sometimes travels to visit other women co-ops. Moreover, in the literature it has been argued that "along with the aforementioned economic, psychological, and social benefits, women's co-operatives may foster women's negotiating skills, as well as their ability to transfer skills to other women co-operators" (Ferguson and Kepe, 2011, 421). There are, however, mixed accounts of this exchange of knowledge and learning from one another in Vakıflı. On the one hand, some of our interviewees emphasize the benefits of working together and learning from each other. For example, one interviewee states the following in this regard: "I'm very good at making bitter orange jam. This is my area of expertise. Another friend of ours makes the walnut jam so perfectly. Today, we are doing pickled oregano in the co-op, for example. One of our friends says she doesn't know how to do it, never done it before. I told her that it was not a problem and that she could learn it from another co-operator. Since it is likely that one of our friends knows it very well. You can observe her, ask her whatever you want, I said. We always support each other. In this way, we include everyone." On the other hand, another interviewee notes the following side of this issue: "Nobody tries to learn what I do. They perhaps think they cannot do what I do. This is typical, isn't it. If there is someone doing something, you just leave it to her. But it is the same for me as well. Whenever I go to the co-op, whatever they do, I roll up my sleeves and help them out. But I cannot make jams so perfectly, I know it." Here, we should note that the issue, as revealed in this specific case, might be related to knowledge asymmetry with the division of labour based on the type of work and expertise required in terms of production, organization of production, and legal/institutional matters. For example, while women can learn from one another different production techniques (requiring a similar knowledge base) with more ease, when a completely different type of knowledge is required (e.g. technical knowledge), it can be a daunting task. In the case of this interviewee, who specializes in technical matters and writing projects for the co-op, the reason for her emphasis on expertise is her expression of the need for perfection, since they cannot tolerate mistakes which would be "too costly," in her words, apart from the fact that technical issues are rather challenging to learn for many. Thus, while participation in women's co-operatives does seem to enable women to have access to new resources and develop relationships, facilitating the dissemination of information and innovative production techniques amongst women (Çınar et al., 2021, 798–799), at the same time, it is not a completely rosy process as the division of labour based on expertise can in certain contexts reinforce knowledge asymmetries. That said, in the case of women's co-op in Vakıflı, all of our interviewees were recognizant of their own expertise, and the extent of their knowledge and its limits; they emphasized the complementarity of each woman's knowledge, and many articulated their openness to learning from others even if this required a lot of extra effort.

To conclude, co-operatives, by their very nature, which stems from the co-operative values that characterize them (e.g. equality, equity, and solidarity), are expected to be gender-sensitive. On the other hand, co-operatives, like other organizational forms, "reflect the broader society in which they operate, and it is therefore not surprising that gender imbalances exist" (Meliá-Marti et al., 2020, 1). It is, nevertheless, possible that "women's co-operatives could be pioneers in creating a new gender discourse in patriarchal and neoliberal societies . . . by enabling economic independence, psychological gains, and social solidarity for their members and standing as an example for other women" (Çınar et al., 2021, 801). Our findings confirm the view that AFNs in general and co-operatives in particular may assume important roles in this regard. Through the activities of the co-op, the women of the village have indeed been going through a positive transformation. Like their counterparts in a diverse range of countries, although these women had little previous experience of participation in AFNs, they have nevertheless managed to become co-operators, revealing that AFNs can and do make a difference in this regard.

Contributions of the co-op to village development and beyond

The advantages of co-operatives are not limited to benefits associated with contributions to their individual members, but they extend to strengthening of the community (Daya and Authar, 2012, 885). In the statements of the members of the women's co-op in Vakıflı, we see a clear emphasis on the importance attributed to the contributions made to the village and its future, in addition to women's livelihoods. What is often seen in the accounts of women is a profound concern and worry about the future prospects of the village, and the possible role the co-op might play in this regard, as, for example, revealed in the following remarks of one founder we interviewed: "Reaching a woman from each house of the village. That was our aim in the beginning, and we did it. This in turn meant of course that the co-op touches every house in the village, we are sure of it."

Moreover, it is repeatedly stated in our interviews that working together in the co-op reinforces the feeling of community and community building. Products, skills and practices, and management of the co-op and hostels are common conversation topics in the village. Apart from the collective work at the co-op, working together in the hostels also provides opportunities for knowledge and skill development. Yet, paralleling the available evidence in the literature, knowledge is not the only thing that is shared. It could be seedlings, or other products and services, including labour (Sato and Soto Alarcón, 2019, 49). The latter is of special importance given that ecological farming requires far more intensive manual labour (Moon, 2022, 11). On the other hand, the countless references to 'togetherness' associated with working in a group include not only work itself but also socializing: "laughing, talking, bringing and sharing food, eating, and drinking," all giving the feeling of a large family, revealed in such statements as "we're like sisters" (Daya and

Authar, 2012, 890). Likewise, in our interviews, the Vakıflı co-op is singled out as a key contributor to the community feeling in the village by enabling villagers to spend a lot of time together. One of our interviewees states the following in this regard: "When you work together, you feel happy. In the end, it is not brain work, and you work with your hands, meaning you can chat at the same time. This then gives way to an environment conducive for making close friendships. Those who wouldn't meet each other otherwise come together in the co-op, and chat. I mean, people that normally wouldn't meet for tea or coffee come together in the co-op and develop friendships while working. The co-op in this way functions as a facilitator for developing social relations in the village." All these accounts confirm the co-ops' role in community development, as "people work together in a co-operative, they build up community identity, establish community norms, learn to trust each other, and commit to providing benefits for each other" (Majee and Hoyt, 2011, 52).

The members of the co-op believe strongly that the co-op improves the village life in many ways. Almost all of them, for example, think that the co-op contributed significantly to the popularity of the village. According to them, the contributions of the co-op in this respect are of particular importance since the village was previously losing even more of its population as a result of migration to urban areas. In the words of one of our interviewees:

> It is impossible to survive in the village if you are not strong economically. What I mean by strong is being self-sufficient really. How are you going to survive in the village without that? There are no other jobs, we create our own jobs in the co-op. The co-op is a kind of employment for us villagers, especially for the women. The women of the village are unlikely to work in Samandağ. Besides, you cannot find any jobs there. It is almost impossible for a woman to find a job in town and commute every day. The co-op gives life to the village in a sense, it is a kind of life buoy.

This is also evident in how the earnings of the co-operative are distributed: as stated earlier, 20% of the earnings is spared for the co-op, mainly to be used for the development of the village, including providing scholarships for university students from Vakıflı. We should perhaps remember at this point that this issue is an important part of the discussions on co-operatives' role in community development, as they "create economic, human, and social capital" (Majee and Hoyt, 2011, 51). It is argued that the emphasis on benefits to the community has been more pronounced in later stages of the co-op in due course (Çameli, 2020). Now, this role has become so important for the co-op that it reveals itself in the accounts of women who much emphasize the role the co-op plays in this regard, as witnessed in the following remarks of one founder we interviewed:

> We tell our youngsters that what we are doing here is to set the foundations. You are the ones that will build the layers on top these

foundations. You should embrace and protect this co-op. Because it is the future of this village. Imagine what would have happened if we hadn't had this women's co-op. I'll tell you, we couldn't have survived this earthquake.

Here, we clearly see that the identification with the co-op in terms of inter-generational continuity of ways of life and village livelihoods is very strong indeed.

The emphasis on community development in the case of the Vakıflı co-op provides further empirical evidence to the line of literature empha-sizing the dual reasoning regarding the main motives for co-operative work and engagement – one being usually political, cultural, and/or ideo-logical, and the other financial and organizational. In some instances, con-tributions to community, be it in the form of anti-mafia activism in Sicily or linked to a globalized movement for the solidarity economy, might be more prevailing (Rakopoulos, 2013, 113). In others, however, motivations for economic empowerment of individual members might be stronger, and there are even instances in which "farmers delivering food to co-operatives are loosely connected with their own communities" (Bilewicz and Śpiewak, 2015, 159). We observe that the emphasis on community development in the case of Vakıflı provides a clear support for the former line of the literature in this regard. Relatedly, as we noted earlier, the importance and prioritization of inclusivity, so that all women can benefit on equal terms by working in the co-op, are other testaments to the community orienta-tion of the Vakıflı co-op, as opposed to a strictly market orientation that would give emphasis to efficiency and profit maximization (Bijman and Wijers, 2019).

Tourism seems to contribute significantly both to the village and to the co-op since it provides a convenient means of selling their products. Visitors' demand indeed constitutes a considerable part of the total sales of the co-op; in fact, it was the most important part before the pandemic and the earthquakes, as mentioned earlier. Moreover, tourism provides a link to the world outside the village. This is a frequently cited benefit of women's co-operatives more generally in that thanks to the co-ops, women learn to reach outside their circles and become part of wider networks, including other co-operatives (Çınar et al., 2021, 795). When asked about whether or not they are in touch with other women's co-operatives, the members of the Vakıflı co-op state that they come together with other co-ops in seminars, workshops, and simi-lar activities. One of our interviewees underlines the important role KEDV played in this regard: "When Sabancı included us, the women's branch of the co-op, in their 'Turkey's Changemakers' series (see Sabancı Vakfı, 2013), I explained them in detail what we do in the co-op. This must have attracted attention. Because, after that KEDV contacted us, they started inviting us to their activities all over the country. I participated in many of these meetings.

I went to İzmir, to Antep, to İstanbul, and learnt a lot about women's co-ops."
Another interviewee states the following in this regard:

> We have good relations with other women's co-ops. For example, we
> bought strawberries from the Yayladağ women's co-op last year. Or when
> we need to consult someone, we call Ms. Nesrin from the Defne women's
> co-op, the most experienced co-op nearby. We have such good relations.
> There was a government body that used to organize meetings of women's
> co-ops from time to time. But after the quakes, they couldn't, they now
> have to reside in a container, trying to re-establish themselves.

In the interviews given to *BirartıBir* (Çameli, 2020), an additional point
underlined by women co-operators in this respect is that, regardless of their
being Arab, Kurdish, Armenian, Orthodox, Sunni, or Alevi, they do connect via
their co-ops and work smoothly together, not even feeling a need to talk about
any cultural or religious differences since they do not matter anymore. In a similar vein, people from different backgrounds might also be reached by many co-
operatives since it is, for instance, possible that co-ops bring together university
graduates and those with primary school diplomas, as we observe in the case
of the Vakıflı co-op, confirming that co-ops are able to "bridge out to women
who are from different classes or ethnic backgrounds" (Çınar et al., 2021, 779).

The 'success' and resilience of the Vakıflı co-op

As we discussed earlier, the social and economic benefits derived from co-
operatives might be significant. The realization of the potential benefits of
co-operatives might also create a self-reinforcing cycle, further increasing the
"confidence in and support for co-operatives as an effective means for organizing the production of agricultural goods and services" (Thomas et al., 2011,
1087). Looking beyond these, it is possible to see even greater roles that co-
ops might assume, including ecological benefits to non-humans, which are of
course "linked to social benefits distributed to co-operative members, members' households, and the larger community including distant consumers"
(Sato and Soto Alarcón, 2019, 50). Given their benefits, a consideration of the
support of the state as well as other national and international organizations
for co-ops is of particular relevance. In Turkey, the governmental support programmes via, for instance, the Ministry of Industry and Trade, the Ministry
of Education, and international organizations such as the UNDP, EU, World
Bank, ILO, and civil society organizations such as KEDV constitute the leading supporting agencies of women's co-operatives (Özdemir, 2013, 302).
This institutional support, however, is seen as unsystematic and unpredictable, often depending on political loyalty, especially at the municipal level.
Just to give an example, Çınar et al. (2021, 787) describe how a co-operative
in Nevşehir "had to vacate the office provided to them by the previous mayor
when a new mayor from a different political party came into office."

We know that as organizations, producer co-ops, although without doubt value economic benefits to their members, do not typically try to grow and maximize profits at all costs. In the case of Vakıflı, limits to growth is evident in the fact that there is a natural boundary in terms of their growth potential: the village. It is, therefore, not uncommon that the co-op turns away customers if the demand exceeds production, rather than trying to expand production beyond the borders of the village. One of our interviewees states the following in this respect: "It is beautiful to be small, neat, and pure; to be special. We don't want our production to be like what you see in a factory. I don't believe that it is possible to generate robust work when there are too many people involved anyway. Neat and pure. We need to see our next step, what exactly we are doing. Otherwise, if we grow too much, we cannot follow what is going on properly. No, it is beautiful like this." Interestingly, BÜKOOP, which is located in the university premises, shares this 'chance' of having a natural boundary with Vakıflı. This careful attitude towards growing beyond the village or the campus, however, does not change the fact that both co-ops would, in fact, like to increase their sales as much as possible. One of our interviewees from Vakıflı even extends this positive attitude with respect to the wish of increasing sales to international sales: "If we manage to get ISO Quality Certificates, we can then try international markets, why not. We know that there is demand for our products from cities like Berlin, for example."

In fact, a different and alternative understanding of growth is shared by these two co-ops, which join forces and co-operate. Small-scale and a 'co-operation of co-operatives' or a 'network of co-operatives' as alternative growth strategies are key choices echoed by many food co-operatives around the world. A recent study of food co-operatives in the Bekaa Valley (Jalkh et al., 2020, 10), for instance, shows that although they are quite small-scale with fewer than 20 members on average, they nevertheless provide evidence that it is possible to develop strategies that "could potentially encourage co-operatives to reorganize in concrete networks to scale up production, highlight product quality, and benefit on a collective level." This is exactly what Vakıflı and BÜKOOP have been trying to accomplish since their relations began in 2009. These relations spanning over 14 years have been quite smooth and exemplary. This has been so despite the fact that the volunteer in BÜKOOP responsible from Vakıflı has changed several times during the course of these long years due to the previously mentioned nature of BÜKOOP being a university-based co-op. Students graduating or faculty members going for a sabbatical make such turnover inevitable, but thanks to the established procedures and systems, up to now, the process of transition has been quite smooth in each and every case. The same is valid for the Vakıflı co-op as well, as evident from the remarks of the following interviewee: "Previously, I was responsible from the relations with BÜKOOP. Until the year 2018, that is. Then, another friend took over. Now, since 2021, a different co-operator is responsible from these orders. We haven't encountered any problems at all. The transition was smooth in each and every case." These warm relations between the two co-ops have peaked in the aftermath of the earthquakes: BÜKOOP volunteers checking and help-ing Vakıflı in all possible ways. There was a meeting of consumer co-ops in Istanbul on 5 March 2023 (about one month after the earthquakes) to discuss how to better organize the ongoing efforts and help producer co-operatives located in the earthquake region. The decision that BÜKOOP should couple with Vakıflı came quite naturally in the meeting. At the time of writing these sentences (July 2023), however, shipment from Vakıflı is still difficult but now possible, at least twice a week.

Another alternative growth strategy, via technology, is also relevant for Vakıflı since it enables the co-op to increase its reach and sales by using online platforms, via ÇiftçidenEve and HepsiBurada web sites in particular. Although online sales are symbolic for the time being, there is a growing trend, especially following firstly the pandemic and then the earthquakes. A limit in this respect is the technical skills required. As men-tioned earlier, the women of the village conduct all work themselves at the co-op, including technical ones, but there is a division of labour given the existing skill levels. "A friend of ours does all the technical things in the co-op, online sales, *etc*. She is a university graduate," explains one of our interviewees. "She knows these things, unlike me. But we don't have to know everything, do we? Perhaps those who know technology so well don't know what I know," she adds, reminding a previous research of ours (Aksoy and Öz, 2020).

We know from the literature that producer co-operatives face severe internal and external challenges, including but not limited to an ageing population, low attraction to the youth, quality-related issues with regard to production, and difficulties in accessing to markets (Jalkh et al., 2020, 10). It has also been underlined that producer co-operatives in general and women's co-operatives in particular face some bottlenecks in Turkey in the areas of finance and legislation, in addition to some internal chal-lenges, such as lack of business skills and expertise in commercial life (Çınar et al., 2021, 790; Duguid et al., 2015, 17; Özdemir, 2013, 303–305). Almost all, if not more, of these overall challenges are faced by Vakıflı as well, together with more specific ones. One of our interviewees, for exam-ple, describes a specific challenge they faced when they wanted to explore the possibility of producing dried fruits by the help of a machine, which indicates the pressing need for support from experts:

We wanted to try a new product category, dried fruits. We bought a machine for this purpose. But we don't know how to use it properly. We don't know the specifics such as how much time, what temperature, *etc* are ideally required for each fruit type. We don't know what to do, we need an expert to give us the necessary information. Now, it is sitting there at the corner of our kitchen. I think it was a bad decision to buy that machine since we don't get any help but I hope I'll be proved wrong.

Another interviewee states that the co-op badly needs a storage space:

> To me, the most important problem of the co-op as of now is that we don't have a storage place. We have to put all the products on top each other, in boxes. We need a kind of depot to properly store our products. This of course needs funding, which means that we have to write another project for this. But I am sure we'll find a solution for it in time.

Yet another challenge, closely resembling a problem observed in several BÜKOOP volunteers, is the issue of burnout. The founder of both the women's branch and the official women's co-op in Vakıflı tells her experience of burnout as follows:

> I am 60 years old now, and I feel very tired from time to time. In 2018, I felt extremely tired, working in the co-op day and night. My feet were aching really bad at the end of each day, and in the end, I got retired. But shortly, I saw that things began to deteriorate. Not followed closely, properly. Seeing that, I decided I couldn't leave the co-op. It is like my baby, you know. I put so much effort, so much energy into its development; it was like raising a child. Now, I am back again. I feel like I should go to the co-op every day. Even if nobody goes, I should go, I feel.

That much commitment, although without doubt admirable, not only poses a real risk of burnout for pioneer co-operators but also challenges the sustainability of co-ops unless established systems that will work independent of certain individuals are put into practice, as we discussed in the case of BÜKOOP.

We have already mentioned in different occasions in this book how not only internal and organizational challenges but also the general state of agriculture and migration to urban areas have had an impact on the co-op and its members. On top of these came the civil war in Syria, a heavy nation-wide economic crisis, a years-long world-wide pandemic, and, most recently, three powerful earthquakes. Still, the villagers are grateful that there were no casualties in Vakıflı. But they fear for the future of their cherished home: "This village is so important for us," explains one of our interviewees, "it is a tiny little village but we are one of the most important colours of Hatay. This village is what is left to us from our ancestors, it is all we have, but I don't really know what will happen to our village in future, whether our youngsters will continue to protect it as we do," she adds. She is joined by other villagers who also express concern regarding future prospects of Vakıflı, especially regarding if the village could survive following the earthquakes or most people will leave and the village will be abandoned, and if it survives, how long it will take to rebuild everything. Hope, however, still persists. "It will all pass, this will also pass," says one of our interviewees who lost her mother who was in nearby Iskenderun during the quakes.

> Our co-op has been therapeutic for us in the aftermath of the quakes, we hold on thanks to our co-op, both economically and psychologically. We forget our troubles when working in the co-op. We prepared product packages for shipment until midnight last March, following the quakes. Everybody supported us. It is like a therapy, working together in the co-op. This co-op kept me on my feet in these difficult times.

In a similar vein, the current head of the women's co-op, after describing how powerless one feels following a catastrophic event of this scale, states that they could find the energy to continue production only because they support each other and, at the same time, feel the support of so many people outside their village.

To summarize, we can say that the expectations of the women of Vakıflı regarding the future prospects of the co-op are generally positive, although their pessimism regarding outward migration to big cities continues. Although they firmly underline that there is a potential role of the co-operative in this respect, they acknowledge that the co-op will not be able to stop the tendency towards urban migration in and of itself given that, in their view, migration is driven not only by economic concerns but also by education-related motives and lifestyle preferences. Moreover, it is a fact that the civil war in Syria and the massive earthquakes of 2023 did not make things any easier for the Vakıflı dwellers. Nevertheless, villagers find their co-op very successful, as evident in the frequently heard statements of our interviewees like "Despite everything, we did it"; "We managed to achieve our goals"; "We succeeded in the end"; *etc*. They in fact see the co-operative as "the most beautiful legacy we can leave to the next generations," in the words of an interviewee. Therefore, although devastating earthquakes significantly damaged many buildings of the village, villagers try to keep their optimism emphasizing their attachment to the village, which they describe lovingly as their 'home.' Despite all odds, in other words, it seems that not only a recovery from the earthquake is on the way in the village of Vakıflı, but there is also a profound hope for a collective future, symbolized by their co-operative.

References

Aksoy, S. (2018). *Türkiye'nin Tek Ermeni Köyü Vakıflı Köyü (Hatay-Samandağ) Üzerine Bir Toplumsal Coğrafya Araştırması*. Unpublished Graduate Thesis, T.C. Van Yüzüncü Yıl Üniversitesi.

Aksoy, Z., & Öz, Ö. (2020). Protection of traditional agricultural knowledge and rethinking agricultural research from farmers' perspective: A case from Turkey. *Journal of Rural Studies*, 80, 291–301. https://doi.org/10.1016/j.jrurstud.2020.09.017

Bijman, J., & Wijers, G. (2019). Exploring the inclusiveness of producer co-operatives. *Current Opinion in Environmental Sustainability*, 41, 74–79. https://doi.org/10.1016/j.cosust.2019.11.005

Bilewicz, A., & Śpiewak, R. (2015). Enclaves of activism and taste: Consumer cooperatives in Poland as alternative food networks. *Socio.hu.*, 3, 145–166. https://doi.org/10.18030/socio.hu.2015en.145

Çameli, T. (Trans. A. Kuryel) (2020). *One for All and All for One: Vakıflı Village Cooperative's Women Branch.* https://birartibir.org/one-for-all-and-all-for-one/ (accessed on 25 February 2023).

Çınar, K., Akyüz, S., Uğur-Çınar, M., & Öncüler-Yayalar, E. (2021). Faces and phases of women's empowerment: The case of women's co-operatives in Turkey. *Social Politics*, 28(3), 778–805. https://doi.org/10.1093/sp/jxz032

Daya, S., & Authar, R. (2012). Self, others and objects in an 'alternative economy': Personal narratives from the Heiveld Rooibos co-operative. *Geoforum*, 43, 885–893. https://doi.org/10.1016/j.geoforum.2012.03.017

Duguid, F., Durutaş, G., & Wodzicki, M. (2015). *The Current State of Women's Co-operatives in Turkey.* The World Bank.

Ferguson, H., & Kepe, T. (2011). Agricultural co-operatives and social empowerment of women: A Ugandan case study. *Development in Practice*, 21(3), 421–429. https://doi.org/10.1080/09614524.2011.558069

Jalkh, R., Dedeire, M., & Desjardins, M. R. (2020). An introduction to food co-operatives in the Bekaa Valley, Lebanon: Territorial actors and potential levers to local development through culinary heritage. *Food Ethics*, 5, 1–18. https://doi.org/10.1007/s41055-020-00079-0

Kopczyńska, E. (2017). Economies of acquaintances: Social relations during shopping at food markets and in consumers' food co-operatives. *East European Politics and Societies and Cultures*, 20(10), 1–22. https://doi.org/10.1177/0888325417710079

Kuşçu, V., & Tuncel, H. (2009). Samandağ'ın (Hatay) organik tarım potansiyeli (organic agricultural potential of Samandağ district (Hatay)). *Fırat Üniversitesi Sosyal Bilimler Dergisi (Fırat University Journal of Social Science)*, 19(2), 43–59.

Liu, P., Gilchrist, P., Taylor, B., & Ravenscroft, N. (2017). The spaces and times of community farming. *Agriculture and Human Values*, 34, 363–375. https://doi.org/10.1007/s10460-016-9717-0

Majee, W., & Ann Hoyt, A. (2011). Co-operatives and community development: A perspective on the use of co-operatives in development. *Journal of Community Practice*, 19(1), 48–61. https://doi.org/10.1080/10705422.2011.550260

McTighe, K. (2018). *Visit Vakıfli, Turkey's Last Armenian Village – Before It Disappears.* www.thedailybeast.com/visit-vakifli-turkeys-last-armenian-villagebefore-it-disappears (accessed on 25 February 2023).

Meliá-Marti, E., Tormo-Carbó, G., & Juliá-Igual, J. F. (2020). Does gender diversity affect performance in agri-food cooperatives? A moderated model. *Sustainability*, 12, 1–27. https://doi.org/10.3390/su12166575

Moon, S. (2022). Women's food work, food citizenship and transnational consumer capitalism: A case study of a feminist food co-operative in South Korea. *Food, Culture & Society*, 25(3), 449–467. https://doi.org/10.1080/15528014.2021.1892255

Oruç, E., Uzunöz, M., & Karadoğan, N. (2017). Rural women's participation of local development: A case of the women shareholders of Vakıflı Development Co-operative. *Asian Journal of Agricultural Extension, Economics & Sociology*, 17(2), 1–12. https://doi.org/10.9734/AJAEES/2017/33435

Özdemir, G. (2013). Women's co-operatives in Turkey. *Procedia – Social and Behavioral Sciences*, 81, 300–305. https://doi.org/10.1016/j.sbspro.2013.06.432

Rakopoulos, T. (2013). Food activism and antimafia cooperatives in contemporary Sicily. In C. Counihan and V. Siniscalchi (eds.) *Food Activism: Agency, Democracy and Economy* (pp. 123–142). Bloomsbury.

Sabancı Vakfı. (2013). *Turkey's Changemakers: Vakıflı Village Women's Co-operative.* Documentary Film. www.youtube.com/watch?v=kDwyrRxNqmM (accessed on 20 January 2023).

Salıcı, A. (2018). Application of ecotourism opportunities spectrum method in ecotourism resources: A case study of Samandağ coastal areas in southern Turkey. *Applied Ecology and Environmental Research*, 16(3), 2701–2715. http://doi.org/10.15666/aeer/1603_27012715

Sato, C., & Soto Alarcón, J. M. (2019). Toward a post-capitalist feminist political ecology's approach to the commons and commoning. *International Journal of the Commons*, 13(1), 36–61.

Thomas, T., Gunden, C., Miran, B., & Manoi, M. A. (2011). Farmers' assessment of social and economic benefits derived from co-operatives, private firms and other agricultural organizations in the Aegean region of Turkey. *Journal of Food, Agriculture & Environment*, 9(3&4), 1085–1087.

4 Conclusions and implications

In this chapter, we first discuss the most salient conclusions derived from the in-depth analysis of two cases from Turkey, namely, BÜKOOP (a consumer food co-op) and Vakıflı (a producer food co-op), with the ultimate purpose of better understanding the challenges of building alternative food networks (AFNs) and possible ways of tackling them. We give a particular emphasis to how these emerging issues resonate at both ends *vis-à-vis* the ideal of empowering the producers and consumers simultaneously. Only then, we proceed to a discussion of the resulting implications of the analysis for the transformative potential of AFNs with regard to achieving a more sustainable and resilient food system.

Facts and possibilities for food co-ops

Gabilondo et al. (2013, 187) write that "as this new century gets underway, the reasons that led to the emergence of cooperativism still exist and in some cases have intensified." Historically troubling questions for co-ops as to how some co-ops manage to survive, whereas others fail; what goals they attain easily and what goals they have to give up (Zwerdling, 1979, 92); what challenges and ambivalences they face; and how they tackle them are still very much alive and relevant today. Inspired by the experiences of BÜKOOP and Vakıflı, we have set to explore challenges of building AFNs in this book, including the dynamics shaping the modes of participation, volunteerism, growth, goal displacement, members' empowerment, and community development in the context of co-operatives. As we demonstrate in the book, the university community at Boğaziçi and the village community in Vakıflı formed strong co-operatives which reveal encouraging evidence that citizens with enthusiasm, perseverance, and hard work can create working models of resilient alternative organizations that aim to provide justice for both producers and consumers.

Acknowledging that 'mission drift' and 'co-operative degeneration' are observed in many co-ops, underlining the difficulty of "the daily implementation of democratic governance principles" (Billiet et al., 2021, 100), our two

DOI: 10.4324/9781003289166-4

case studies with their maintained balance with regard to 'dreams/ideals' and 'practical necessities' of running an organization provide valuable evidence. We learn from the cases of BÜKOOP and Vakıflı that significant challenges and tensions can indeed emerge in food co-ops between 'ideals' and 'practical necessities,' which might provide fruitful results if managed well. Curiously, as highlighted by Mooney (2004), inevitable frictions associated with different dimensions of co-operation can also become sources of innovation and flexibility. We should perhaps repeat here that the possible transformative role of such tensions is particularly emphasized by the volunteers of BÜKOOP, providing further supporting evidence for "the disruptive potential of the underlying frictions" (Fonte and Cucco, 2017, 301).

Moreover, such tensions might also carry a potential to reveal very fundamental undercurrents such as the class dimension. For example, in the case of a consumer co-operative, the objective of guaranteeing a fair price to producers might be in conflict with the objective of offering affordable products to all, not only to upper and middle-class consumers. If the consumer co-op offers a diverse price range for a single product category as a remedy, this might in turn generate an unintended consequence, encouraging competition between producers (Vastenaekels and Pelenc, 2018). Just to give a related example, a couple of years ago, when a prominent figure from Vakıflı learnt that BÜKOOP procures tangerines from another producer from Bodrum (an area known for its particular variety of tangerines), the associated feelings were rather intense: "I am really disappointed to hear that, our tangerines won international prizes, why don't you buy them from us instead," he protested. The explanation was simply a matter of taste in this instance, whereas in other occasions it might be related to other factors such as the price of the product. In fact, it is not rare for BÜKOOP to carry alternatives of the same product (e.g. this is the case for olive oil and honey), a practice which does not only serve to cater taste differences but also offer a price range for consumers in line with the above-stated objective of offering affordable products for all.

The case of Vakıflı provides additional insights regarding this issue, which, for example, manifest itself in some unintended consequences of participatory decision-making. As detailed in Chapter 3, last year, the decision about how much pomegranate syrup to produce was taken by a majority vote, despite the fact that the women co-operators in the board of directors knew from experience that the agreed amount would probably not be sufficient. The result is that this year the syrup has been sold out as of June. Having seen this, co-op members have 'learnt by doing' to hear more carefully what the more experienced members of the co-op have to say regarding a particular issue, and they intend to make their future decisions taking this into account. It is important to note here that nobody in the co-op argues for giving up the 'ideal' of participatory decision-making as a result of such 'accidents,' but they try to find workable, constructive solutions instead. Overall, BÜKOOP and Vakıflı continually struggle to balance the demands of the co-operative process and practical necessities of running an organization, and this duality of idealism–pragmatism is, in fact, inherent in their identities resembling other food co-ops (Ashforth and Reingen, 2014). Their style of managing the tension generated by this duality is, on the other hand, particularly inspiring in that it seems to provoke a lively debate to find solutions in each and every case of conflict, instead of producing a split between 'idealists' and 'pragmatists.'

It has been argued in the literature that food co-ops have been more faithful to the original spirit of the co-operative movement, making decisions collectively and providing a forum for progressive communities to practice how they could build alternative networks (McGrath, 2004). We have been, at the same time, warned that there is a "need to continuously interrogate what co-operation is in action," since otherwise "if an intentional process of co-operation is not sought after, it can be easy to revert back to the competitive values that drive traditional economic processes, even under the banner of a co-operative legal form. Projects working deliberately on organizational and interactional aspects of co-operation may fare better in creating better food futures – an aspiration that fuelled steps toward co-operation in the first place" (Hale and Carolan, 2018, 131). Although "the cooperativeness of co-operatives is often assumed in practice," in other words, legal status alone does not guarantee co-operative relationships (Hale and Carolan, 2018, 130). In addition to the essential process of participatory decision-making, collective work and fair sharing of the workload are also crucial for avoiding power asymmetries, which can lead to alienation and disillusionment on the part of co-op members. Even in instances when particular types of knowledge, such as expertise on information technologies or project writing, are held by one or few members, as we see in the case of Vakıflı, when these members actively take part in the everyday work of the co-op (making jams, syrups, *etc.*), the value of complementarity of different types of knowledge required to make the co-op work becomes much more visible to them. The importance of "individual and private communications and conversations taking place during mundane and repetitive activities" (Liu et al., 2017, 372) should not be underestimated in this regard. We have repeatedly seen in this book that doing practical work together is of supreme importance for both BÜKOOP and Vakıflı. We further learn from these two cases that working collectively is considered as the key in creating and maintaining co-op spirit by the co-op members, which, according to them, serves as a type of 'glue' and a reference point. Volunteers consider building a co-op spirit collectively as a real achievement of both BÜKOOP and Vakıflı. This co-op spirit is continuously kept alive, triggering a process of restructuring if needed (like it did in the case of Vakıflı). Thus, we also learn from these two cases that this spirit does not necessarily deteriorate over time. This is crucial as in the opposite scenario "the deterioration of members' loyalty and commitment may eventually endanger the very existence of a co-operative because members' participation lies at the heart of any member-based organization" (Bhuyan, 2007, 277).

The therapeutic potential and role of both BÜKOOP and Vakıflı for their members are much pronounced as well. For the volunteers of BÜKOOP, active and participatory membership brings benefits well beyond access to healthy food as theorized in the literature (Liu et al., 2017, 373) – volunteers frequently mentioning how happy and emotionally fulfilled they feel while in the co-op. Likewise, the members of the Vakıflı co-op repeatedly underline the therapeutic role of the co-op for them, which has become even more obvious in the aftermath of the earthquakes. The members of the Vakıflı co-op state that working in the co-op together after the quakes 'saved' them psychologically. More generally, the contributions of the co-op to women's economic and social empowerment as well as the feelings of satisfaction and proud stemming from owning their own income and making contributions to their families and community are also particularly noteworthy. In addition, the very decision of the women's branch to turn into an independent co-op to equally benefit all women participating in the endeavour, the learning process within the co-op, and the contribution the women's co-op makes to sustain livelihoods in the village at a time when only agricultural production and tourism could not meet the needs of village dwellers anymore are all crucial indicators of the importance of co-operatives in fostering community development. Here, various forms of capital, be it financial, human, and social capital, developed through practices women engage within the co-op demonstrate the role co-ops can play particularly in bonding, but also through enabling them to meet and network with other women co-ops, showing the potential for further bridging social capital, which has important implications for women's empowerment and community development (Çınar et al., 2021; Ajates, 2021).

Another set of findings derived from the two cases we studied concerns the benefits associated with the direct link between the consumers and producers, in both a physical and an emotional sense. Direct links and shorter supply chains do seem to have an advantage, especially in times of crisis. A comparison of the impact of the pandemic on long and short food supply chains in the US and Turkey, for instance, reveals that "Turkey experienced fewer disruptions in the supply chain," and in both countries, AFNs that rely on "strong mechanisms of consumer–producer trust" and on "reduced physical and emotional distance between producers and consumers" proved more resilient (Abiral and Atalan-Helicke, 2020, 227; 234–235). Such a direct link, amongst other things, has the potential to enable consumers and producers to conduct plans together to ensure a sustainable and predictable supply and demand. BÜKOOP, for example, keeps regular and detailed statistics and shares them with producers on a yearly basis so that they can know in advance the likely demand from BÜKOOP for their products. The members of Vakıflı co-op underline that this information – that is, being in the know regarding the potential demand for their products – is of prime importance for them. The lessons that can be derived from a focus on the mutual relation of these two co-ops also include the fact that open communications and mutual trust play key roles in maintaining a good long-term relationship. Here, a related question is whether establishing multi-stakeholder co-operatives (MSCs) can provide a productive ground for creating more sustainable food flows between rural and urban areas. The long-term engagement of both co-ops; the flow of information about not only amounts for supply and demand but also knowledge about the product, how it is produced and by whom; and sustained interaction between volunteers and members responsible for contact between co-ops all point to the potential for creating 'third spaces' where active involvement of both producers and consumers in a process of continual dialogue about major decisions to be taken and reflexively come up with innovative ideas is a possibility (Ajates Gonzales, 2021, 17). Therefore, we wish to ask whether the establishment of an MSC can provide an opportunity to strengthen this relationship already existing between the two co-ops by formalizing this 'third space.'

The analysis of BÜKOOP and Vakıflı as 'small in scale but large in prospect' organizations also raises important points about the ambivalence of 'small is beautiful.' In fact, demonstrating that food co-ops do not need to expand outside of their boundaries to survive (whether it is a village or a university campus) is a key contribution afforded by the analysis of BÜKOOP and Vakıflı. Anderson et al. (2014, 4) note that an important characteristic of co-operative AFNs is the "emergent forms of collective action that are reoriented towards democratic principles," in contrast to the "large-scale, profit-oriented marketing co-operatives, . . . which have lost much of their dynamism and emancipatory potential." Evidence from Italian co-ops further suggests that tensions and challenges are more manageable for smaller co-operatives and for those "operating in disadvantaged and marginal rural areas where co-operatives may be key actors in developmental alliances with other local agricultural and not-agricultural actors" (Fonte and Cucco, 2017, 301).

Relatedly, progressive scholars have been criticized for being seduced by small scale (e.g., Samers, 2005). Bernardi (2007, 15), for instance, argues that "large and successful co-operatives do not necessarily stop being 'good' co-operatives," and large scale is "not always accompanied by a loss of cultural and democratic values." Put aside the fact that we do need to hear about such experiences, we should perhaps clarify that the experience of BÜKOOP in this respect reveals not only that 'small is beautiful' but also that 'it is not sufficient' since, in order to reach a scale that makes a difference for producers, the need for a network organization of co-ops is repeatedly underlined. According to Billiet et al. (2021), the necessity of such a bond amongst co-operatives "is further strengthened by the fundamental co-operative principle of 'collaboration among co-operatives,' which encourages co-operatives to seek out co-operative suppliers, customers, and employees to conduct their activities, as well as to participate in sectoral and geographical (both national and international) networks of co-operatives" (ICA, 2015, cited in Billiet et al., 2021, 103). This is also linked to the issue of embeddedness of co-operatives in a global movement (Billiet et al., 2021, 103–104). Moreover, solidarity amongst co-operatives is argued "to be further reinforced in times of crisis as a sort of defence mechanism to preserve the co-operative organizational model and values, and to find collective solutions to keep satisfying the needs of co-operatives' members" (Billiet et al., 2021, 104).

Overall, given also that the challenges of keeping co-op values while expanding have been well acknowledged in the literature (Flecha and Ngai, 2014), 'small BÜKOOP' and 'small Vakıflı' are indeed beautiful when internal advantages, especially with regard to building a capacity to continually produce co-op spirit via working closely together, are considered. But these two cases also reveal that small scale is not sufficient and, hence, warn us against the trap of fetishization of scale (Born and Purcell, 2006; Brown and Purcell, 2004). In this way, we are forced to confront the question of whether or not setting solid, working models of alternative organizations is enough. We have seen that the kind of economic organization that BÜKOOP tries to shape in co-operation with small producers, including Vakıflı, will only reach an economically meaningful scale when actors join forces and build enough bargaining strength. Efforts to unite food co-ops, however, are quite challenging since there might be divisions between those who believe in the need for a federation and those who prefer autonomous local co-ops with loose links with other co-ops (Balnave and Patmore, 2012, 990). Whether the links are strong or weak, this alternative understanding of growth, that is, growing via a 'co-operation amongst co-operatives,' might be a challenge to achieve in practice (Sumner et al., 2014), as we further discuss in the following section.

AFNs and the sustainability of food systems: Any hope for transformation?

Co-operatives are value-based and principle-driven organizations and, by their very nature, should include sustainable and participatory mechanisms. As such, they "are well-placed to contribute to sustainable development's triple bottom line of economic, social, and environmental objectives" (ILO and ICA, 2014, 4). Specifically, food co-operatives are highly relevant to and might potentially help achieve many sustainable development goals (SDGs) like poverty reduction (Jalkh et al., 2020, 4) and food security and natural resource management. The potential of the contribution that co-operatives can make to the realization of SDGs, nevertheless, is argued to be not visible enough at neither the national nor the international level (ILO and ICA, 2014, 16). Our analysis of BÜKOOP and Vakıflı in this book provides a contribution in this respect given that the importance attributed by these two co-ops to the above-stated SDGs is very pronounced, as shown throughout the book, be it with regard to their overall attempts for the development of a just food system or towards community development as well as women's economic and social empowerment. In terms of environmental sustainability, on the other hand, the focus of BÜKOOP to work with producers who engage in sustainable production processes, including the use of local or traditional varieties of seeds, which is extremely important for the conservation of agricultural biodiversity as Anatolia is the centre of genetic diversity for several important crops, including wheat (Karagöz and Zencirci, 2005), and controlled use of chemical inputs, and Vakıflı co-op's processing syrups and jams of local varieties of fruits (most notably, pomegranate) through a careful mix of traditional and modern techniques with minimum negative impact on the environment are crucial contributions that need to be emphasized.

We know from the literature that co-operatives have proven resilient in times of economic and financial crises (ILO and ICA, 2014, 4). Specifically, two main characteristics of co-ops are seen as rendering them resilient. Firstly, since their focus is on satisfying members' needs, "co-operatives will tend to continue their production or service delivery for their members in times of crisis to sustain their needs, livelihoods, and well-being." Secondly, their being firmly embedded both in a global movement and in local communities enables them to re-arrange their priorities when necessary so that they could support their communities in difficult times (Billiet et al., 2021, 100–103). In recent years, the response and initiatives of the AFNs to the crisis induced by the pandemic have been argued to be successful because they "were able to continue their distribution under serious lockdown and mobility restrictions during the initial months of COVID-19 due to the diversity of producers within their networks, their flexibility in procurement and distribution, and the ability of their producers to use household labour. They were also able to adapt quickly and respond to disruption" (Atalan-Helicke and Abiral, 2021, 91). In a similar vein, Billiet et al. (2021) argue that during the COVID-19 crisis, "the bond between co-operatives and members was strengthened in both directions: members supported their co-operatives, and co-operatives supported their members to get through the crisis" (Billiet et al., 2021, 103). These contentions in the literature are supported by the evidence provided in this book. We have seen in Chapter 2 the specifics of how remarkable a resilience BÜKOOP has shown when faced with a series of crises in recent years, including but not limited to the pandemic. Likewise, we have seen in Chapter 3 that the Vakıflı co-op has both survived itself and helped its members and thus the village community to survive in many diverse ways in the face of severe subsequent crises, the most recent one being the February 2023 earthquakes. It indeed seems that a "member-centred mission and their self-help values, democracy, and solidarity," which prevail in these two co-ops, might prove very useful in times of crises (Billiet et al., 2021, 105).

Digitalization of food co-operatives, which became all the more crucial with the pandemic, is another important issue (Cristobal-Fransi et al., 2020; Jorge-Vázquez et al., 2021). In the case of BÜKOOP, although information and communication technologies are essential for the smooth handling of internal operations (e.g. via emails, WhatsApp, and Dropbox) and marketing of the products (e.g. via Facebook, Twitter, and Instagram), refusing online sales has been this co-op's philosophy since the beginning, and this principle has not changed during the pandemic, mainly to maintain the much-cherished co-op spirit. This position, at the same time, highlights the fact that consumer food co-ops are about much more than food. Otherwise, it would be perfectly possible to access, say, organic food, in regular supermarkets or via online platforms. This also relates to Sarmiento's (2017, 487) point about "the pedagogic capacities (or at least potentials) of AFNs" with their focus on how engagement in these networks enables participants to develop a reflective framework about food that "ultimately allow them to develop a deeply felt, embodied knowledge through which to become more aware of issues such as food insecurity and inequality of access to healthy foods, producer livelihood struggles, and the ecological and human health implications of particular foods and diets" (Sarmiento, 2017, 487). As such, broader benefits of food co-ops include "experiencing the spaces and times in which community is performed through embodied and material practices" (Liu et al., 2017, 372), and that is exactly why BÜKOOP is rather sceptical about online sales. The only technology-related change during the pandemic in BÜKOOP was the decision to accept credit cards, as mentioned in Chapter 2. Regarding producer co-ops, on the other hand, the trend towards digitization, which had already been underway for many in the pre-pandemic era, has been even more pronounced. Vakıflı, for instance, had already begun selling its products via online platforms before the pandemic, but these were very limited in scale. However, as discussed in Chapter 3, the pandemic has accelerated this trend significantly. This, of course, brings about another dimension of the issue, which relates to the capacity of food co-ops to support such technological changes. The women's co-op in Vakıflı is lucky to have a member equipped with the required technological skills who moved from Istanbul to the village and took the responsibility regarding online sales and relations, revealing the likely influence of 'key individuals' and 'chance events' in developing such a capacity. For those co-ops that are not as lucky to have a member (or members) with developed technological skills, however, this issue might pose a real challenge.

The experiences of the two co-ops analysed in this book speak volumes to the transformative role and potential of food co-ops, and how they might go so much beyond providing 'just another option in the market.' In this regard, questioning whether or not and to what extent AFNs, including food co-operatives, remodel fundamental relations in the dominant food system is crucial: "Failing that, whatever their originality, their magnitude, or their generosity, they are in danger of being captured by the very same system they claim to leave behind and becoming accomplices – without their knowledge – to what they denounce or reject" (De Leener and Totté, 2017, 220, cited in Vastenaekels and Pelenc, 2018, 26). That is why "the extent to which food co-operatives challenge these fundamental relations and help transform the economy with their values and ethics" is of particular concern (Vastenaekels and Pelenc, 2018, 26). There is thus a pressing need for empirical works detailing the specifics of the transformative role of food co-ops (Cajka and Novontny, 2022), and the cases of BÜKOOP and Vakıflı analysed in this book enable us to muse about this exact issue: Whether/how food co-ops could provide a framework for transformation of the dominant food system.

A line of the relevant literature discusses the question of "how such sparse micro-alternatives may organize themselves in such a way as to constitute a sufficient transformative force" (Vastenaekels and Pelenc, 2018, 27). Put another way, we may ask if there are any ways food co-ops could gain enough economic strength to challenge the dominant food system. Yes, some argue, if they join forces to form large networks "that consolidate their wholesale orders, build more and larger warehouses, and create interstate trucking networks" (Zwerdling, 1979, 107). Efforts to unite food co-ops, however, are seen as quite challenging since, as we noted earlier, there might be divisions between federalists and individualists (Balnave and Patmore, 2012, 990), and they may not share the same political or philosophical visions and goals. There are those believing that "politics in a food co-op are irrelevant," while others might argue that the ultimate purpose of food co-ops is precisely politics (Zwerdling, 1979, 108), all this in turn echoing the classical Marxist stand that views co-ops in isolation as a decoy, or trap, but when they join forces to form a federation, they could then be seen as transition forms (Lorenzo, 2013, 84). A related concern is the high probability that co-ops if they combine forces are likely to make a difference and hence attract competitive attention (Balnave and Patmore, 2012). We know from the literature that this might even lead to a process in which co-operatives are transformed into business firms (Levi and Davis, 2008, 2184), returning us once again to the issue of goal displacement, so much discussed in both cases we analysed in this book.

There is also the view that setting solid, working models of alternative organizations is not enough since alternative forms can be transformed and adopted by the dominant system (Guthman, 2008), again reaching the familiar question regarding co-ops' ability to offer a real challenge or a genuine 'alternative' to the existing food system. Maintaining a non-confrontational manner, which is a key priority for many AFNs, is similarly associated with the risk of mainstreaming of food politics (Si et al., 2015, 309). This is argued to be already "well reflected in the global spread of ethical or political consumption, as well as the explosive growth of 'organic' or 'local' food marketing and consumption" (Moon, 2022, 449). Views that co-operatives are not really distinguishable from capitalist firms, that co-operatives are short-lived, and that the co-operative sector is insignificant and thus unthreatening to the dominant economic order are also frequently stated (Gibson-Graham, 2003, 136).

And yet, isn't it a fact that with all their problems and ambivalences, the very existence of co-ops like BÜKOOP and Vakıflı poses a solid challenge to "the *necessity* of what has become normalized" (Paranque and Willmott, 2014, 618) as the dominant food system? Recalling Rosol's (2020, 59) emphasis on alternative economic practices, including economic transactions such as compensated prices for students (BÜKOOP); working practices such as voluntary labour (BÜKOOP); and forms of economic organization such as co-operatives (BÜKOOP; in the case of Vakıflı, we expressly see the will to form an official co-operative to ensure equal inclusion of all women), the cases we analyse do point to the agency of individuals and collectives to initiate change. We have seen in this book that to better understand whether or not alternatives to the dominant food system are 'successful,' we need to focus our analytical lens not only on structure and its deterioration but also on organizational processes. Co-operatives as a species of organization are constituted by their members, and thus, success of the co-op in this sense should be seen as the manifestation of an ongoing process of production and re-production of the co-op spirit by these very members, echoing the re-production perspective (Stryjan, 1994). This perspective has its roots in Giddens (1984) and DiMaggio and Powell (1983) and assigns a central role to individual members' inputs in constituting a social system. Mooney (2004, 92) aptly notes that "no longer seen as merely a means to a given end, the means and ends of co-operation are fused; or stated differently, the process of co-operation prefigures an interest or value in the co-operation itself as an objective that inheres in the very process of co-operating." As such, we wish to underline once again that *co-operatives as an organizational form within AFNs* have the most potential to be founded upon democratic principles, shared knowledge, equality in participation and decision-making, alternative economic transactions, and community orientation that can push forward and transform the dominant food system in a way that addresses injustices and inequalities created by this very system itself.

As discussed in detail in Chapters 2 and 3, the experiences of BÜKOOP and Vakıflı do not only challenge the notion of 'success' but also, as 'successful' alternative organizations in their own terms, they provide evidence against the familiar pessimism about alternative organizations and contribute to the debate on alternative food movements by pointing to the possibility of establishing co-operative organizations as an alternative to the dominant food system that continually works to overcome many of the shortcomings associated with these initiatives. What resonates in such pessimism in fact has its roots in the first systematic studies of co-operatives; the degeneration thesis of Fabian socialists in the 19th century, for example, envisages an inevitable process of deterioration that ultimately leads to economic failure and/or a loss of democratic characteristics in worker co-operatives (Stryjan, 1994, 61). Most unfortunately, this pessimism generates a conceptualization that causes one to postpone their dreams for a better world to an uncertain future. But thankfully, as Rothschild (2016, 29) underlines, some people are already trying to create a better life, investing their time and efforts to making ideas that might seem utopian real (Hoffmann, 2016, 168). The cases of BÜKOOP and Vakıflı discussed in this book are working examples providing evidence against this pessimism about alternative food movement in general and food co-ops in particular. As we demonstrate in the book, although challenges are significant, achievements of both co-ops are very inspiring. These co-ops in particular have fulfilled their initial goal of empowering the consumer and producer ends simultaneously. As food co-ops "constitute an institutionalized form of interaction between consumers and farmers, which is 'co-produced' by both of them" (Jaklin et al., 2015, 44), the establishment of some degree of control over agricultural production and consumption process is without doubt a crucial step towards providing an alternative to the dominant food system.

Needless to say, as Paranque and Willmott (2014, 620) state, whether alternative structures would be able to transform the dominant food system will only be seen in time. At this point, the role food co-ops *can* play in altering dominant forms of the linkage between agricultural production as the starting point and consumption as the final stage becomes all the more pertinent, particularly in the context of neoliberal transformation that has characterized governance of agriculture and food. We know that some urban food co-ops see themselves as social and political catalysts for progressive groups and movements such as the farmer unions and the ecological movement. On the production side, for example, Stock et al. (2014, 413) emphasize the notion of 'actual autonomy' and view co-operative efforts based on collectivism that simultaneously aim 'social and environmental goals' as distinct from 'neoliberal autonomy,' characterizing co-operative efforts which operate according to the logic of the market. In this context, a question is whether strong links between such farmer-led co-operatives that aim towards actual autonomy and urban food co-operatives can provide important impetus for the possibility of alternative forms of agricultural production and mechanisms of distribution and consumption, which are ecologically sustainable and socially just for both producers and consumers. An important caveat here would be to differentiate mechanisms such as payments for ecosystem services (PES) and organic labelling, which are market-based from a holistic approach to agriculture and food, which views agriculture as a livelihood and respects rural identities that are manifested in farmers' control over their production process (Stock et al., 2014). This also relates to the discussion on AFNs in the Global North and South in terms of their role in respective food systems. The analysis of BÜKOOP and Vakıflı shows the limits of organic certification mechanisms that AFNs in the North use as a crucial component of developing alternative practices, which is aptly criticized for reproducing neoliberal rationalities. On the production side, Vakıflı and other producers that BÜKOOP works with are strong manifestations of the importance of place-based, agro-ecological practices which local producers, in harmony with nature, engage in sustainable production but cannot afford to get organic certification for. On the consumer side, BÜKOOP actively supports these producers, simultaneously aiming at affordable and healthy food for its members. Yet, we also need to note that this is a continual process of interaction and learning, as there have been instances when a university member is shopping from BÜKOOP, questioning whether the products sold are organic or not. This is not unique to BÜKOOP, as other AFNs in Istanbul face similar challenges in that not all AFN members are interested in the production process or farmers' wellbeing but mostly look for healthy food for themselves. This is a similar challenge that AFNs in both the North and the South face, as the discussion Lamine et al. (2012) provide in the context of France and Brazil shows. Relatedly, according to Stock et al., the emphasis on actual autonomy "creates an opening in theoretical and political dialogue to bridge concerns about the implications of neo-liberalization of nature for farmers, livelihood, and environmental outcomes without resorting to typical dichotomies between North and South, peasant versus family versus other kinds of farmers and other unhelpful distinctions" (Stock et al., 2014, 421). Therefore, while acknowledging the differences of the contexts that AFNs operate, a strict North–South divide is not necessarily accurate; in fact, there is perhaps a lot that AFNs in the North can learn from the experience of AFNs in the South in terms of building solid and working rural–urban relations, and *vice versa*.

To conclude, the analysis of BÜKOOP and Vakıflı presented in this book provides evidence to be hopeful regarding the transformative potential of AFNs in general and food co-operatives in particular. Co-operative volunteers see their hope in acting, 'here and now' rather than postponing their dreams to an uncertain future. Food co-ops in this sense could be seen as future-oriented organizations, "aiming to create what is often termed a 'politics of possibility.' Seeking to open up the usually critical gaze of scholarship 'to possibility rather than limits on the possible'" (Gibson-Graham, 2008, 614). Whether the dream for a better world is "crafted through the formation of solidarity economies linking co-ops, environmentalists, social movement groups, local governments, and others into an alternative system of production and exchange or by means of a powerful political party, we will arrive at such a world through work, education, politicization, and persuasion," Healy (2015, 353) argues. We as scholars can, in addition, contribute towards this undertaking by making alternatives more visible and participating as theorists and practitioners in building them (King and Learmonth, 2014, 17). We believe the experiences of BÜKOOP and Vakıflı provide valuable contributions in this respect.

References

Abiral, B., & Atalan-Helicke, N. (2020). Trusting food supply chains during the pandemic: Reflections from Turkey and the U.S. *Food and Foodways*, 28(3), 226–236. https://doi.org/10.1080/07409710.2020.1790147

Ajates, R. (2021). Reducing the risk of co-optation in alternative food networks: Multi-stakeholder co-operatives, social capital, and third spaces of co-operation. *Sustainability*, 13, 11219. https://doi.org/10.3390/su132011219

Anderson, C. R., Brushett, L., Gray, T., & Renting, H. (2014). Working together to build co-operative food systems. *Journal of Agriculture, Food Systems, and Community Development*, 4(3), 3–9. https://doi.org/10.5304/jafscd.2014.043.017

Ashforth, B. E., & Reingen, P. H. (2014). Functions of dysfunction: Managing the dynamics of an organisational duality in a natural food co-operative. *Administrative Science Quarterly*, 59(3), 474–516. https://doi.org/10.1177/0001839214537811

Atalan-Helicke, N., & Abiral, B. (2021). Alternative food distribution networks, resilience, and urban food security in Turkey during the COVID-19 pandemic. *Journal of Agriculture, Food Systems, and Community Development*, 10(2), 89–104. https://doi.org/10.5304/jafscd.2021.102.021

Balnave, N., & Patmore, G. (2012). Rochdale consumer co-operatives in Australia: Decline and survival. *Business History*, 54(6), 986–1003. https://doi.org/10.1080/00076791.2012.706899

Bernardi, A. (2007). The co-operative difference: Economic, organisational and policy issues. *International Journal of Co-operative Management*, 3(2), 11–22.

Bhuyan, S. (2007). The 'people' factor in co-operatives: An analysis of members' attitudes and behaviour. *Canadian Journal of Agricultural Economics*, 55, 275–298. https://doi.org/10.1111/j.1744-7976.2007.00092.x

Billiet, A., Dufays, F., Friedel, S., & Staessens, M. (2021). The resilience of the co-operative model: How do co-operatives deal with the COVID-19 crisis? *Strategic Change*, 30, 99–108. https://doi.org/10.1002/jsc.2393

Born, B., & Purcell, M. (2006). Avoiding the local trap: Scale and food systems in planning research. *Journal of Planning Education and Research*, 26, 195–207. https://doi.org/10.1177/0739456X06291389

Brown, J. C., & Purcell, M. (2004). There's nothing inherent about scale: Political ecology, the local trap, and the politics of development in the Brazilian Amazon. *Geoforum*, 36, 607–624. https://doi.org/10.1016/j.geoforum.2004.09.001

Cajka, A., & Novontny, J. (2022). Let us expand this Western project by admitting diversity and enhancing rigor: A systematic review of empirical research on alternative economies. *Ecological Economics*, 196, 107416. https://doi.org/10.1016/j.ecolecon.2022.107416

Cristobal-Fransi, E., Montegut-Salla, Y., Ferrer-Rosell, B., & Daries, N. (2020). Rural co-operatives in the digital age: An analysis of the internet presence and degree of maturity of agri-food co-operatives' e-commerce. *Journal of Rural Studies*, 74, 55–66. https://doi.org/10.1016/j.jrurstud.2019.11.011

Çınar, K., Akyüz, S., Uğur-Çınar, M., & Öncüler-Yayalar, E. (2021). Faces and phases of women's empowerment: The case of women's co-operatives in Turkey. *Social Politics*, 28(3), 778–805. https://doi.org/10.1093/sp/jxz032

De Leener, P., & Totté, M. (2017). Transitions économiques: En finir avec les alternatives dérisoires. Ed. du Croquant.

DiMaggio, P. J., & Powell, W. (1983). The iron cage revisited: Institutional isomorphism and collective rationality in organisational fields. *American Sociological Review*, 48(2), 147–160. https://doi.org/10.2307/2095101

Flecha, R., & Ngai, P. (2014). The challenge for Mondragon: Searching for the co-operative values in times of internationalisation. *Organization*, 21(5), 666–682. https://doi.org/10.1177/1350508414537625

Fonte, M., & Cucco, I. (2017). Co-operatives and alternative food networks in Italy. The long road towards a social economy in agriculture. *Journal of Rural Studies*, 53, 291–302. https://doi.org/10.1016/j.jrurstud.2017.01.019

Gabilondo, L. A., Idiakez, A. L., & Tricio, E. P. (2013). Mondragon: The dilemmas of a mature cooperativism. In C. P. Harnecker (ed.) *Co-operatives and Socialism: A View from Cuba* (pp. 167–189). Palgrave MacMillan.

Gibson-Graham, J. K. (2003). Enabling ethical economies: Cooperativism and class. *Critical Sociology*, 29(2), 123–161. https://doi.org/10.1163/156916303769155788

Gibson-Graham, J. K. (2008). Diverse economies: Performative practices for 'other worlds'. *Progress in Human Geography*, 32(5), 613–632. https://doi.org/10.1177/0309132508090821

Giddens, A. (1984). *The Constitution of Society*. University of California Press.

Guthman, J. (2008). Neoliberalism and the making of food politics in California. *Geoforum*, 39, 1171–1183. https://doi.org/10.1016/j.geoforum.2006.09.002

Hale, J., & Carolan, M. (2018). Cooperative or uncooperative cooperatives? Digging into the process of cooperation in food and agriculture cooperatives. *Journal of Agriculture, Food Systems, and Community Development*, 8(1), 113–132. https://doi.org/10.5304/jafscd.2018.081.011

Healy, S. (2015). Communism as a model of life. *Rethinking Marxism*, 27(3), 343–356. https://doi.org/10.1080/08935696.2015.1044358

Hoffmann, E. A. (2016). Emotions and emotional labour at worker-owned businesses: Deep acting, surface acting, and genuine emotions. *The Sociological Quarterly*, 57, 152–173. https://doi.org/10.1111/tsq.12113

ICA (2015). *Guidance Note to the Co-operative Principles*. Brussels: International Co-operative Alliance.

ILO & ICA. (2014). *Co-operatives and the Sustainable Development Goals: A Contribution to the Post-2015 Development Debate a Policy Brief*. ILO & ICA.

Jaklin, U., Kummer, S., & Milestad, R. (2015). Why do farmers collaborate with a food co-operative? Reasons for participation in a civic food network in Vienna, Austria. *The International Journal of Sociology of Agriculture and Food*, 22(1), 41–61. https://doi.org/10.48416/ijsaf.v22i1.136

Jalkh, R., Dedeire, M., & Desjardins, M. R. (2020). An introduction to food co-operatives in the Bekaa Valley, Lebanon: Territorial actors and potential levers to local development through culinary heritage. *Food Ethics*, 5(20), 1–18. https://doi.org/10.1007/s41055-020-00079-0

Jorge-Vázquez, J., Chivite-Cebolla, M. P., & Salinas-Ramos, F. (2021). The digitalisation of the European agri-food co-operative sector. Determining factors to embrace information and communication technologies. *Agriculture*, 11(6), 514. https://doi.org/10.3390/agriculture11060514

Karagöz, A., & Zencirci, N. (2005). Variation in wheat (*Triticum* spp.) landraces from different altitudes of three regions of Turkey. *Genetic Resources Crop Evolution*, 52, 775–785. https://doi.org/10.1007/s10722-004-3556-3

King, D., & Learmonth, M. (2014). Can critical management studies ever be 'practical'? A case study in engaged scholarship. *Human Relations*, 68(3), 353–375. https://doi.org/10.1177/0018726714528254

Lamine, C., Darolt, M., & Brandenburg, A. (2012). The civic and social dimensions of food production and distribution in alternative food networks in France and Southern Brazil. *International Journal of Sociology of Agriculture and Food*, 19(3), 383–401. https://doi.org/10.48416/ijsaf.v19i3.211

Levi, Y., & Davis, P. (2008). Co-operatives as the 'enfants terribles' of economics: Some implications for the social economy. *The Journal of Socio-Economics*, 37, 2178–2188. https://doi.org/10.1016/j.socec.2008.06.003

Liu, P., Gilchrist, P., Taylor, B., & Ravenscroft, N. (2017). The spaces and times of community farming. *Agriculture and Human Values*, 34, 363–375. https://doi.org/10.1007/s10460-016-9717-0

Lorenzo, H. M. (2013). Cooperativism and self-management in Marx, Engels, and Lenin. In C. P. Harnecker (ed.) *Co-operatives and Socialism: A View from Cuba* (pp. 63–89). Palgrave MacMillan.

McGrath, M. (2004). That's capitalism, not a co-op: Countercultural idealism and business realism in 1970s U.S. food co-ops. *Business and Economic History On-line*, 2, 1–14. www.thebhc.org/publications/BEHonline/2004/McGrath.pdf

Moon, S. (2022). Women's food work, food citizenship, and transnational consumer capitalism: A case study of a feminist food co-operative in South Korea. *Food, Culture & Society*, 25(3), 449–467. https://doi.org/10.1080/15528014.2021.1892255

Mooney, P. H. (2004). Democratizing rural economy: Institutional friction, sustainable struggle and the co-operative movement. *Rural Sociology*, 69(1), 76–98. https://doi.org/10.1526/003601104322919919

Paranque, B., & Willmott, H. (2014). Co-operatives – saviours or gravediggers of capitalism? Critical performativity and the John Lewis Partnership. *Organization*, 21(5), 604–625. https://doi.org/10.1177/1350508414537622

Rosol, M. (2020). On the significance of alternative economic practices: Reconceptualizing alterity in alternative food networks. *Economic Geography*, 96(1), 52–76. https://doi.org/10.1080/00130095.2019.1701430

Rothschild, J. (2016). The logic of a co-operative economy and democracy 2.0: Recovering the possibilities for autonomy, creativity, solidarity, and common purpose. *The Sociological Quarterly*, 57, 7–35. https://doi.org/10.1111/tsq.12138

Samers, M. (2005). The myopia of 'diverse economies,' or a critique of the 'informal economy'. *Antipode*, 37(5), 875–886. https://doi.org/10.1111/j.0066-4812.2005.00537.x

Sarmiento, E. R. (2017). Synergies in alternative food network research: Embodiment, diverse economies, and more-than-human food geographies. *Agriculture and Human Values*, 34, 485–497. https://doi.org/10.1007/s10460-016-9753-9

Si, Z., Schumilas, T., & Scott, S. (2015). Characterizing alternative food networks in China. *Agriculture and Human Values*, 32, 299–313. https://doi.org/10.1007/s10460-014-9530-6

Stock, P. V., Forney, J., Emery, S. B., & Wittman, H. (2014). Neoliberal natures on the farm: Farmer autonomy and co-operation in comparative perspective. *Journal of Rural Studies*, 36, 411–422. https://doi.org/10.1016/j.jrurstud.2014.06.001

Stryjan, Y. (1994). Understanding co-operatives: The reproduction perspective. *Annals of Public and Co-operative Economics*, 65(1), 59–80.

Sumner, J., McMurtry, J. J., & Renglich, H. (2014). Leveraging the local: Co-operative food systems and the local organic food co-ops network in Ontario, Canada. *Journal of Agriculture, Food Systems, and Community Development*, 4(3), 47–60. https://doi.org/10.5304/jafscd.2014.043.004

Vastenaekels, J., & Pelenc, J. (2018). *Investigating the Potential of Co-operatives to Re-embed the Economy: A Multiple Case Study of Food Co-operatives in Belgium.* Working Paper CIRIEC No. 2018/05. Universite de Liege.

Zwerdling, D. (1979). The uncertain revival of food co-operatives. In J. Case & R. J. R. Taylor (eds.) *Co-ops, Communes & Collectives: Experiments in Social Change* (pp. 89–111). Pantheon Books.

Index

Adaman 18
Agricultural Reform Implementation
    Project (ARIP) 14
agro-tourism 11
auto-ethnography 21
Ahi movement 15–16
Ajates Gonzales, R. 12
alienation 10, 30, 34, 39, 40, 69
Alkon, A. H. 6
Allen, P. 5
alternative food networks (AFNs):
    categorization 5–6; criticism
    6; definitions 4; networks
    1–7; pedagogic capacities 74;
    practices 7; role in Global
    North 13; role in Global South
    13; pessimism 1, 2, 76–77;
    transformative potential 7, 12,
    14, 67–68, 74, 78; Turkey 14–
    22; typology 6; women's roles
    11; see also co-operatives
Anderson, C. R. 7
Anderson et al. 6, 71
Antakya 1; see also Hatay
Atasoy, Y. 14
Aydın Fig Producers Company 16
Aysu, A. 18

Ballı, E. 17, 18
Bellante, L. 13
Bijman, J. 12
Biocoop 7
Boğaziçi Members Consumer Co-
    operative (BÜKOOP): approach
    to growth 38–42, 61, 71–72;
    benefits 70–71; challenges
    14, 31–34, 42–44, 62, 67–78;
    community development
    12; emotional debts 43;
    establishment 1, 28–29; fair

prices 32; flexibility 36; history
    28–34; mutual trust 34–35, 42;
    online sales 73–74; organic
    certification 13, 30–31, 42;
    organizational development
    29–30, 40–43, 75–78; PGS
    certification scheme 30–31, 35;
    pre-payment system 32, 33;
    student discounts 32; success/
    resilience 14, 34, 37–44,
    72–78; tension 8, 14, 34–37,
    68–69; therapeutic role 70;
    trust-based relationships 31–32;
    volunteerism 28–44
Brazil 13, 78
burnout 10, 42–43, 63

Chen, K. K. 10
Çınar, K. 60
class 11, 13, 21, 68
collectivist work 10, 39
commons 35
community development 11–12, 14,
    57–60
competition 4, 6, 8, 18, 68
co-operatives: challenges 4–5, 8–14,
    67–68; contributions 72–78;
    definition 2–3; evolution 5, 7;
    flexibility 8, 36, 41, 68, 73;
    organizational development
    9–10, 75–78; roles 4–5;
    structure 9–10; transformative
    potential 7, 12, 14, 67–68,
    74, 78; women's roles 11; see
    also alternative food networks
    (AFNs)
co-operative degeneration 67, 76
co-op spirit 2, 7, 9, 10, 14, 29, 37, 38–40,
    44, 69, 72, 74, 76
country chests 16

COVID-19 pandemic 15, 22, 31–32, 34, 51, 52, 59, 62, 63, 70, 73–74
Craig, G. 5

decision-making 37, 38, 52–53, 55, 68–69, 76
de-growth 2, 3, 8–9
Demirkılıç, S. 14
DiMaggio, P. J. 76
direct relationship 5, 9, 14, 15, 31, 34–35, 40, 44, 70
Duguid, F. 20
Duncan, J. 6–7

economic empowerment 54–56
eco-tourism 48

fair prices 4, 7, 12, 13, 16, 18, 33, 38, 44, 68
Farmers' Union 41
Feenstra, G. W. 4
food price inflation 14–15
Forssell, S. 4
Foundation for the Support of Women's Work (KEDV) 50, 59
France 7, 13, 78
Furman, C. A. 40

Gabilondo, L. A. 67
Gibson-Graham, J. K. 2, 4
Giddens, A. 76
Global North 3, 13, 77, 78
Global South 3, 4, 13, 14, 77, 78
goal displacement 36, 67, 75; *see also* co-operative degeneration; mission drift
Gödence co-operative 31
Gonzales, V. 11
Goodman et al. 4
Gritzas, G. 5, 35
Guthman, J. 6

Haedicke, M. A. 8
Hatay 47, 48, 50, 63; *see also* Antakya
Healy, S. 78
Hergesheimer, C. 5
Hopa Tea Co-operative 19
Hoyt, A. 11

inequality 6, 74
International Co-operative Alliance (ICA) 3, 11
International Labour Organization (ILO) 11

International Panel of Experts on Sustainable Food Systems (IPES) 3
Istanbul 1, 15, 28, 29, 42, 47, 50, 52, 60, 62, 74, 78
Izmir 19, 20, 31, 60

Japan 7
Jarosz, L. 4

Kadıköy Co-op 15
Kadirbeyoglu, Z. 15
Kaya, C. 41–42
Kavoulakos, K. 5, 35
Kaynar, I. S. 18
knowledge 6, 9, 10, 15, 30, 51, 53, 56–57, 69, 71, 74, 76
Konya, N. 15

labour 4, 6, 8, 10, 11, 19, 37, 40, 43, 49, 51, 56, 57, 62, 73, 76
Lamine, C. 78
Lankoski, L. 4
Leach, D. K. 10
Little et al. 7, 36
localism 4, 6, 8, 14, 15, 30–31, 40, 41, 44, 50, 71, 72, 73, 75, 77
Lund, M. 12

Majee, W. 11
Mansbridge, J. J. 10
Mares, T. M. 6
market competition 8
marketing 16, 49, 71, 74, 75
methodology 21–22
Mexico 11, 50
middle class 13, 68
migration 22, 47, 49, 52, 58, 63, 64
mission drift 67
Moon 11, 55, 57
Mooney, P. H. 8, 29, 68, 76
multi-stakeholder co-operatives (MSCs) 2, 12, 71
mutual trust 34–35, 42

neighbourhood co-ops 15, 28, 38, 42
neoliberalism 2, 6, 14, 77
new generation co-operatives 19
new wave co-ops 7

Okan and Okan 16, 17, 18, 20
online sales 52, 62, 73–74
organic certification 13, 30–31, 42, 48, 77

organic labelling 77
Ovacık Agricultural Development Co-
operative 19
Özçay Co-operative 19
Özdemir 20, 21, 60, 62

Papavasiliou, F. 40
Paranque, B. 77
Parkins, W. 5
participatory certification 13
participatory guarantee systems (PGS)
13, 30–31, 35
Pascucci, S. 6–7
payments for ecosystem services (PES) 77
Philips, R. G. 11
Powell, W. 76
power 10, 30, 37, 69
producer–consumer relations 5, 15, 19, 42
product information form 30–31

Qazi, J. A. 5

Renting, H. 5
Rosol, M. 7, 29, 76
Rothschild, J. 76
Rothschild-Whitt, J. 9–10

Şahin, C. E. 19
Sarmiento, E. R. 5, 74
Sato, C. 11
Schneider, F. 8–9
Seikatsu Club 7
Selfa, T. L. 5
shipment 33, 39, 43, 52, 62, 64
short food supply chains (SFSCs) 5
Sicily 59
social capital 11, 12, 58, 70
Soto Alarcón, J. M. 11
Soysal Al 15, 42, 44
Stock, P. V. 77
sustainable de-growth 8–9
sustainable development goals (SDGs) 72
sustainability 41, 49, 63, 72–73
Syria 22, 63, 64

Tariş (union of fig producers) 16
technological skills 9, 62, 69, 73–74
tension 1–2, 8, 9, 12, 14, 71
Tire Milk Producers Development
Co-operative 19
tourism 11, 47–48, 52, 59, 70
Tregear, A. 5
trust-based relationships 5, 15, 31–32,
35, 37, 38, 41, 42, 58, 70–71

Turkey: agricultural production 14–15;
alternative food networks
14–22; Boğaziçi Members
Consumer Co-operative 1,
12, 13, 14, 28–44, 61, 62,
67–78; governmental support
programmes 60; history of
co-operatives 14–22; legal
framework of co-operativism
16–17; Union of Hazelnut
Sales Co-operatives 18;
Vakıfköy Women's Enterprise,
Production, and Management
Co-operative 1, 11, 12, 13,
47–64, 67–69; women's co-
operatives 19–21

Vakıfköy Women's Enterprise,
Production, and Management
Co-operative (Vakıflı co-op):
approach to growth 61,
71–72; benefits 54–56, 70–71;
challenges 14, 62, 67–69;
community development 12,
14, 57–60; establishment 1, 49;
history 47–53; online sales 52,
62, 74; organic certification 13;
organizational development
40–41, 51–53, 75–78;
pre-payment system 51; role
in women's empowerment 11,
14, 53–57; success/resilience
14, 60–64, 72–78; tension 8,
14, 68–69; therapeutic role 53,
64, 70
Vakıflı Village Agro-Development Co-
operative (Vakıflı agriculture
co-op) 1, 49–50
volunteerism 8, 10, 12, 28–44, 51, 61–62,
63, 67, 68, 69–70, 78

Watts, D. C. H. 5
Wertheim, E. G. 30
WhatsApp 38
Wijers, G. 12
Willmott, H. 77
Wittman, H. 5
women's co-operatives 19–21; *see also*
Vakıfköy Women's Enterprise,
Production, and Management
Co-operative (Vakıflı co-op)
World Bank 14, 15, 20

Zitcer, A. 7

For Product Safety Concerns and Information please contact our EU
representative GPSR@taylorandfrancis.com
Taylor & Francis Verlag GmbH, Kaufingerstraße 24, 80331 München, Germany

www.ingramcontent.com/pod-product-compliance
Lightning Source LLC
Chambersburg PA
CBHW061837220326
41599CB00027B/5309